REFLECT ⁴

REFLECT⁴
LISTENING & SPEAKING

PAUL DUMMETT

Australia • Brazil • Mexico • Singapore • United Kingdom • United States

National Geographic Learning,
a Cengage Company

Reflect 4 Listening & Speaking
Author: Paul Dummett

Publisher: Sherrise Roehr
Executive Editor: Laura Le Dréan
Development Editor: Lisl Bove
Director of Global Marketing: Ian Martin
Product Marketing Manager: Tracy Baillie
Senior Content Project Manager: Mark Rzeszutek
Media Researcher: Jeffrey Millies
Art Director: Brenda Carmichael
Senior Designer: Lisa Trager
Operations Coordinator: Hayley Chwazik-Gee
Manufacturing Buyer: Mary Beth Hennebury
Composition: MPS Limited

For permission to use material from this text or product, submit all requests online at **cengage.com/permissions**
Further permissions questions can be emailed to **permissionrequest@cengage.com**

Student Book ISBN: 978-0-357-44914-1
Student Book with Online Practice: 978-0-357-44920-2

National Geographic Learning
200 Pier 4 Boulevard
Boston, MA 02210

Locate your local office at **international.cengage.com/region**

Visit National Geographic Learning online at **ELTNGL.com**
Visit our corporate website at **www.cengage.com**

Printed in Mexico
Print Number: 01   Print Year: 2021

SCOPE AND SEQUENCE

 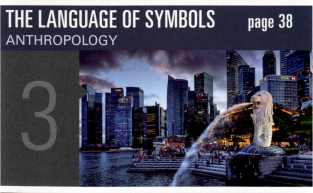

SPEAKING & PRONUNCIATION	GRAMMAR	CRITICAL THINKING	REFLECT ACTIVITIES
Check understanding and clarify Reductions in questions	Direct and indirect questions	Apply prior knowledge	▶ Compare your home to someone else's ▶ Evaluate changes to your childhood home ▶ Discuss connections to places ▶ **UNIT TASK** Interview someone about a place they belong
Report findings and conclusions Consonant clusters containing -s	Modals	Justify an opinion	▶ Consider cultural influences ▶ Assess cases of cultural borrowing ▶ Discuss influences on languages ▶ **UNIT TASK** Report on borrowed words in your language
Refer to visuals in a presentation Commonly confused vowel sounds	Past perfect	Make reasonable judgments	▶ Describe artworks of historical importance ▶ Discuss the meaning of symbols ▶ Discuss symbols you use to communicate ▶ **UNIT TASK** Design and present a new symbol
Use rhetorical questions Rhythm and stress	Unreal conditionals	Summarize	▶ Discuss the role of science in our lives ▶ Imagine scientific possibilities ▶ Describe devices that appear in science fiction ▶ **UNIT TASK** Present a significant breakthrough

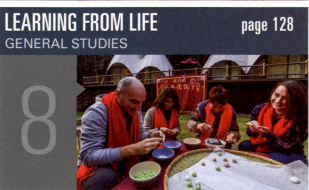

SPEAKING & PRONUNCIATION	GRAMMAR	CRITICAL THINKING	REFLECT ACTIVITIES
Present a balanced view Stress in words with suffixes	The passive voice	Make a balanced judgment	▶ Evaluate the amount of plastic in our lives ▶ Consider how plastic waste can be reduced ▶ Consider disadvantages to green solutions ▶ **UNIT TASK** Present arguments for and against a green idea
Define and explain a concept Linking between vowel sounds	Quantifiers	Interpret statistics	▶ Consider how a company can affect people's lives ▶ Analyze data about social enterprise ▶ Interpret statistics about disabilities ▶ **UNIT TASK** Present a social enterprise
Make constructive comments Contrastive stress	Connectors	Follow a line of reasoning	▶ Describe your emotions ▶ Analyze your emotional intelligence ▶ Consider ways of handling emotions ▶ **UNIT TASK** Use your emotional intelligence
Ask for clarification Thought groups and pausing	Noun clauses	Be aware of the whole picture	▶ Discuss challenges for students entering a new school ▶ Reflect on important transitions in life ▶ Compare the value of education and experience ▶ **UNIT TASK** Share a memorable learning experience

CONNECT TO IDEAS

Reflect Listening & Speaking features relevant, global content to engage students while helping them acquire the academic language and skills they need. Specially-designed activities give students the opportunity to reflect on and connect ideas and language to their academic, work, and personal lives.

National Geographic photography and content invite students to investigate the world and discuss high-interest topics.

Watch & Speak and **Listen & Speak** sections center on high-interest video and audio that students will want to talk about as they build academic listening and speaking skills.

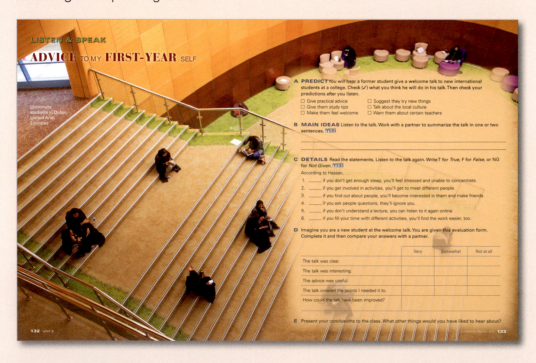

CONNECT TO ACADEMIC SKILLS

Frieda and Diego Rivera by Frida Kahlo

COMMUNICATION TIP

When we describe a picture, we use the present continuous to say what we can see happening in it. We use the verbs *seem* and *appear* to express what we think may be happening:

A woman is holding some flowers.
There's a man (who is) looking out of the window.
The woman appears to be nervous.
Note that we don't use *seem* and *appear* in the continuous form.

C Listen to someone talk about *Frieda and Diego Rivera*. Discuss the questions with a partner.

1. Who is the painting of?
2. What is the woman wearing?
3. What does the bird represent?
4. What does the painting suggest about the relationship?

D Listen to part of the description of the painting again and complete the paragraph. Use one or two words in each blank.

He's in a suit and ¹_____ his paintbrushes. ²_____ a bird ³_____ over them—a dove, I think—which I suppose represents peace. But it's not a typical, happy wedding portrait. ⁴_____ to be other messages in it.

REFLECT Describe artworks of historical importance.

You are going to watch a video about the significant discoveries of Genevieve von Petzinger, a paleoanthropologist (someone who studies the origins of humans using fossils and other artifacts), cave art researcher, and National Geographic Explorer. Think of a painting, sculpture, monument, or other piece of art that is important in your country's history. Then work in a small group. Describe your choice and:

▸ What it represents
▸ Why it is important

THE LANGUAGE OF SYMBOLS **41**

Scaffolded activities build confidence and provide students with a clear path to achieving final outcomes.

Reflect activities give students the opportunity to think critically about what they are learning and check their understanding.

SPEAKING SKILL   Ask for clarification

When you listen to a description or explanation, you may need to check that you've understood the information properly. You can do this by highlighting the point and then asking for clarification. You should never be afraid to ask for clarification. Use phrases and questions such as:

I didn't quite get what you said about . . .
I didn't follow the part about . . .
I'm not sure I understood an expression you used.
When you said . . ., what (exactly) did you mean by that?
Could you explain/say a bit more about . . .?
Could you give an example?

M APPLY Listen again to the last part of the model. One of the people in the audience asks a question about something he didn't understand. Complete the question and answer.

B: Thank you for sharing that. It sounds amazing. There was just one thing I ¹_____. You said that you learn when you do things that are outside of your comfort zone. What ²_____?

A: Well, ³_____ certain tasks or assignments feel really easy to complete? That's because they're in your comfort zone. They feel familiar and safe. Things that are outside of your comfort zone can make you feel a little uncomfortable. ⁴_____ I grow a lot when I need to take a risk and do something new or different.

N APPLY Work with a partner. Look at the statements below. Take turns asking and answering questions about the words and phrases in bold to check understanding. Use a dictionary to look up any words you don't know.

> My favorite teacher was a **substitute teacher** we had for one semester.

> We had to do a project that involved interviewing **health care workers**.

> I made a model of an airplane out of **Plasticine**, and I was so proud of it.

> I was bad at drawing, so the teacher said I could **make a collage** instead.

LEARNING FROM LIFE **143**

Focused academic **listening** and **speaking skills** help students communicate with confidence.

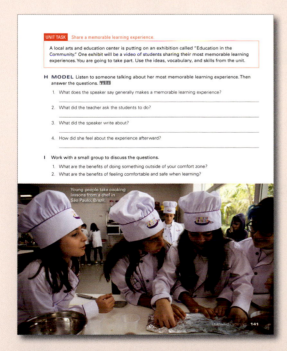

UNIT TASK Share a memorable learning experience.

A local arts and education center is putting on an exhibition called "Education in the Community." One exhibit will be a video of students sharing their most memorable learning experiences. You are going to take part. Use the ideas, vocabulary, and skills from the unit.

H MODEL Listen to someone talking about her most memorable learning experience. Then answer the questions.

1. What does the speaker say generally makes a memorable learning experience?
2. What did the teacher ask the students to do?
3. What did the speaker write about?
4. How did she feel about the experience afterward?

I Work with a small group to discuss the questions.

1. What are the benefits of doing something outside of your comfort zone?
2. What are the benefits of feeling comfortable and safe when learning?

Young people take cooking lessons from a chef in São Paulo, Brazil.

LEARNING FROM LIFE **141**

O PLAN Take notes in the chart below about your most memorable learning experience. Think carefully about what you are going to say.

Where and when did it happen?	
What did you have to do?	
How did you feel beforehand?	
What made it a special experience?	
What did you learn?	
How did you feel afterward?	

P PRACTICE Describe your learning experience to a partner. Use pauses to make your description sound clear and natural. Ask your partner for feedback to help you with the final presentation.

Q UNIT TASK Share your most memorable learning experience with the class. Answer any questions. Be sure to ask your classmates questions about anything you don't understand in their presentations. Then vote on which experiences should be sent to the exhibition. Use the criteria below or create your own.

▸ Most unusual
▸ Most fun
▸ Biggest lesson learned
▸ Best outcome

144 UNIT 8

Clear models, relevant grammar, and step-by-step planning give students the support they need to complete the final speaking task successfully.

CONNECT TO ACHIEVEMENT

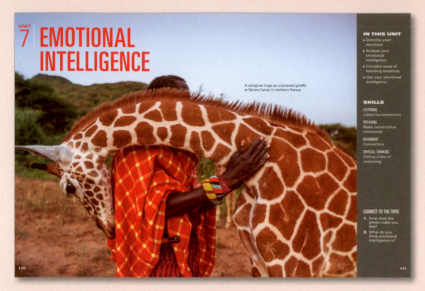

Reflect at the end of the unit is an opportunity for formative assessment. Students review the skills and vocabulary they have gained.

DIGITAL RESOURCES

TEACH lively, engaging lessons that get students to participate actively. The Classroom Presentation Tool helps teachers to present the Student's Book pages, play audio and video, and increase participation by providing a central focus for the class.

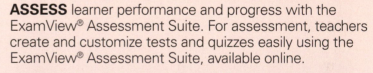

LEARN AND TRACK with Online Practice and Student's eBook. For students, the mobile-friendly platform reinforces learning through additional practice. For instructors, progress-tracking is made easy through the shared gradebook.

ASSESS learner performance and progress with the ExamView® Assessment Suite. For assessment, teachers create and customize tests and quizzes easily using the ExamView® Assessment Suite, available online.

ACKNOWLEDGMENTS

The Authors and Publisher would like to acknowledge the teachers around the world who participated in the development of *Reflect*.

A special thanks to our Advisory Board for their valuable input during the development of this series.

ADVISORY BOARD

Dr. Mansoor S. Almalki, Taif University, Saudi Arabia; **John Duplice**, Sophia University, Japan; **Heba Elhadary**, Gulf University for Science and Technology, Kuwait; **Hind Elyas**, Niagara College, Saudi Arabia; **Cheryl House**, ILSC Education Group, Canada; **Xiao Luo**, BFUS International, China; **Daniel L. Paller,** Kinjo Gakuin University, Japan; **Ray Purdy**, ELS Education Services, USA; **Sarah Symes,** Cambridge Street Upper School, USA.

GLOBAL REVIEWERS

ASIA

Michael Crawford, Dokkyo University, Japan; **Ronnie Hill**, RMIT University Vietnam, Vietnam; **Aaron Nurse**, Golden Path Academics, Vietnam; **Simon Park**, Zushi Kaisei, Japan; **Aunchana Punnarungsee**, Majeo University, Thailand.

LATIN AMERICA AND THE CARIBBEAN

Leandro Aguiar, inFlux, Brazil; **Sonia Albertazzi-Osorio**, Costa Rica Institute of Technology, Costa Rica; **Auricea Bacelar**, Top Seven Idiomas, Brazil; **Natalia Benavides**, Universidad de Los Andes, Colombia; **James Bonilla**, Global Language Training UK, Colombia; **Diego Bruekers Deschamp**, Inglês Express, Brazil; **Josiane da Rosa**, Hello Idiomas, Brazil; **Marcos de Campos Bueno**, It's Cool International, Brazil; **Sophia De Carvalho**, Ingles Express, Brazil; **André Luiz dos Santos**, IFG, Brazil; **Oscar Gomez-Delgado**, Universidad de los Andes, Colombia; **Ruth Elizabeth Hibas**, Inglês Express, Brazil; **Rebecca Ashley Hibas**, Inglês Express, Brazil; **Cecibel Juliao**, UDELAS University, Panama; **Rosa Awilda López Fernández**, School of Languages UNAPEC University, Dominican Republic; **Isabella Magalhães**, Fluent English Pouso Alegre, Brazil; **Gabrielle Marchetti**, Teacher's House, Brazil; **Sabine Mary**, INTEC, Dominican Republic; **Miryam Morron**, Corporación Universitaria Americana, Colombia; **Mary Ruth Popov**, Ingles Express, Ltda., Brazil; **Leticia Rodrigues Resende**, Brazil; **Margaret Simons**, English Center, Brazil.

MIDDLE EAST

Abubaker Alhitty, University of Bahrain, Bahrain; **Jawaria Iqbal**, Saudi Arabia; **Rana Khan**, Algonquin College, Kuwait; **Mick King**, Community College of Qatar, Qatar; **Seema Jaisimha Terry**, German University of Technology, Oman.

USA AND CANADA

Thomas Becskehazy, Arizona State University, AZ; **Robert Bushong**, University of Delaware, DE; **Ashley Fifer**, Nassau Community College, NY; **Sarah Arva Grosik**, University of Pennsylvania, PA; **Carolyn Ho**, Lone Star College-CyFair, TX; **Zachary Johnsrud**, Norquest College, Canada; **Caitlin King**, IUPUI, IN; **Andrea Murau Haraway**, Global Launch / Arizona State University, AZ; **Bobbi Plante**, Manitoba Institute of Trades and Technology, Canada; **Michael Schwartz**, St. Cloud State University, MN; **Pamela Smart-Smith**, Virginia Tech, VA; **Kelly Smith**, English Language Institute, UCSD Extension, CA; **Karen Vallejo**, University of California, CA.

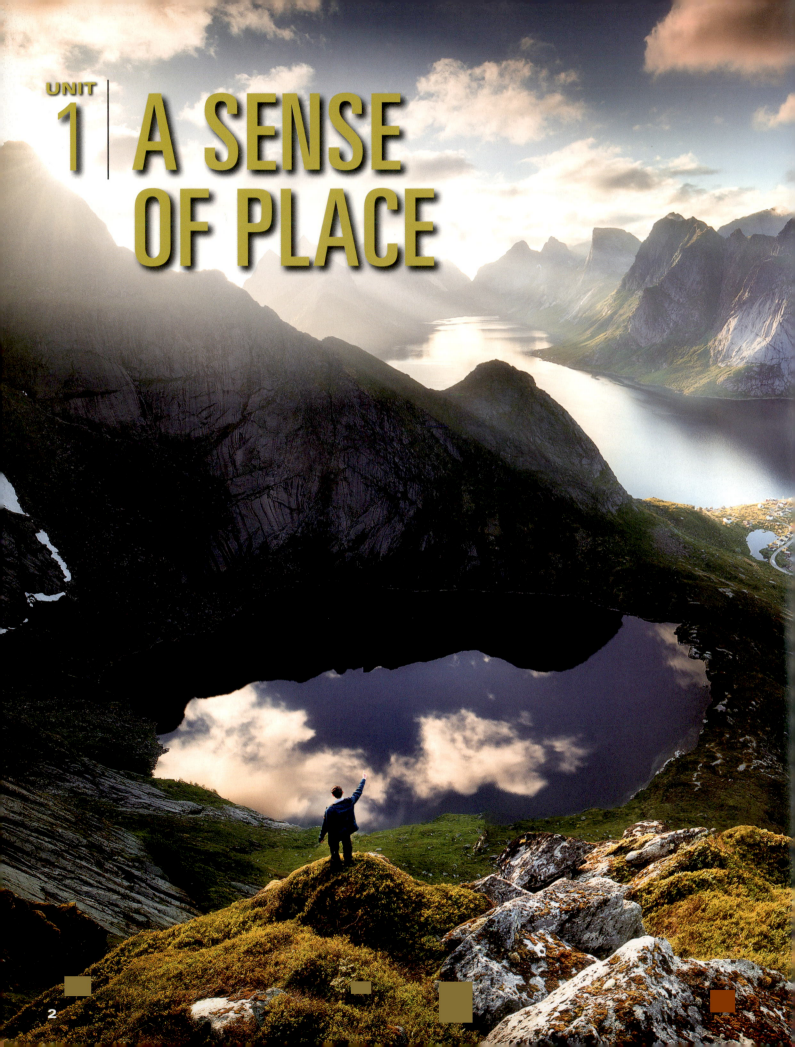

A SENSE OF PLACE

The Lofoten Islands, Norway

CONNECT TO THE TOPIC

1. Describe the place in the photograph.
2. What do you think connects people to this place?

3

PREPARE TO WATCH

A **VOCABULARY** Listen to the words in bold. Then discuss the meaning of these words with a partner. 🎧 1.1

1. Living on my own was a shock at first, but I'm slowly beginning to **adapt**.

2. It's a very old house, but it has all the modern **conveniences**, like central heating and Wi-Fi.

3. In New Zealand we start to **harvest** grapes in late February, when the fruit is ready.

4. Fishing is my **livelihood**. I don't know what I'd do if I didn't have a boat.

5. Farming didn't pay well, so they had to look for other **means** of making money.

6. They **rely on** their cars because there's no public transportation.

7. **Survival** in the wilderness requires knowledge and skills.

8. This town has seen a **transformation** since the factory was built and more people moved in.

9. My **typical** day begins with a light breakfast. It's what I always do.

10. It's great that he's **utilizing** his skills as a builder to help the local community.

B Match the words from activity A with the correct definitions.

1. _____ adapt (v)   a. a big change

2. _____ convenience (n)   b. to depend on

3. _____ harvest (v)   c. to make or accept changes

4. _____ livelihood (n)   d. a thing that makes life easier

5. _____ means (n)   e. how you make money

6. _____ rely on (v phr)   f. to make practical use of

7. _____ survival (n)   g. methods; ways

8. _____ transformation (n) h. usual

9. _____ typical (adj)   i. to collect food or crops

10. _____ utilize (v)   j. staying alive

C You will hear someone talking about where different members of their family live. Listen and complete each part of the chart with one word. 🎧 1.2

Family member(s)	Place	Type of home	Description
Parents	Staten ¹_____ in New York	²_____ clapboard house	Quiet, ³_____, has a slower pace of life; becoming more ⁴_____
Cousins	Bolzano, ⁵_____	⁶_____	⁷_____ region in the north; pretty, ⁸_____ city

D PERSONALIZE Work with a partner. Describe a place where one of your family members lives. Take notes in your notebook before you speak, using the headings in the chart in activity C.

REFLECT   Compare your home to someone else's.

You're going to watch a video about how Inuit hunters in Greenland live. Work with a partner. Ask each other questions about where you live. What is the same? What is different?

▸ What type of home do you live in? (house, apartment)
▸ How old is your home?
▸ How many people live there?
▸ How long have you lived there?
▸ What area is your home in? (in the city, country)
▸ Do you have any outdoor space? (garden, yard)

The Staten Island Ferry in New York, USA, connects Staten Island to Manhattan.

A CHANGING WORLD

A PREVIEW Work with a partner. Look at the photo and read the caption. Have you heard of the Inuit? If so, what do you know about Inuit hunters?

B MAIN IDEAS Watch the video. Choose the correct answers. ▶ 1.1

1. In what ways are the Inuit hunters' lives changing?

   a. They are unable to hunt now.

   b. They are hunting in different ways now.

2. What is the attitude of the hunters to this change?

   a. They aren't very happy about the change.

   b. They are excited about the new possibilities.

Inuit fishermen at the mouth of the Ilulissat Icefjord near Ilulissat, Greenland

When you listen to a talk or watch a report, it's important to notice the speaker's tone of voice. The tone of a speaker's voice often helps to indicate his or her attitude. Listen for the speaker's pitch and intonation.

▸ Is the speaker loud? (angry or excited) Or quiet? (calm)
▸ Is their intonation flat? (a bit negative or uninterested)
▸ Does their intonation rise and fall? (positive or interested)

C APPLY Listen to one hunter talk about the effect climate change will have on their livelihoods. Write the adjectives that best describe his tone of voice and attitude. Then share your ideas with a partner. 🎧 1.3

D DETAILS Read the questions. Then watch the video again and choose the correct answers. ▶ 1.1

1. Which of these things are not a common sight in Greenland anymore?

   a. Seals and whales

   b. Dogs and sleds

2. How was Inuit life simpler in the past?

   a. They had no electricity.

   b. They didn't need dogs.

3. What did the first hunter say that appeared to show a positive attitude?

   a. He can hunt alone.

   b. He can hunt all year.

4. What is the second hunter worried about?

   a. His son will leave home.

   b. There will be nothing to do.

5. What problem is the narrator describing?

   a. The Inuit will not survive here.

   b. The Inuit will have to change.

6. What difference between hunting with dogs and with a boat does the third hunter mention?

   a. The noise

   b. The speed

E Work with a partner. Complete the paragraph with the correct form of the words.

| adapt | conveniences | harvest | rely on | survival | transformation |

In the past, there were no modern ¹_____ like power tools.

The Inuit ²_____ their dogs and their skills as hunters for

³_____. Now they're using boats to ⁴_____

fish from the sea. The Inuit will ⁵_____ to the new way of life,

but it means a ⁶_____ in the way they hunt.

F The life of Inuit hunters is closely connected to the land and sea. Work with a partner to make a list of five other jobs that are connected to a particular place. Share your list with the class.

GRAMMAR   Direct and indirect questions

Indirect questions put a question inside another question such as *Can you explain . . .?* or *Do you know . . .?* This type of question is often more polite.

Direct questions
Where does he live?
Is it very cold there in the winter?

Indirect questions
Can you tell me <u>where he lives</u>?
Do you know <u>if it is very cold there in the winter</u>?

Note: The original question (the question inside the other) has statement word order. We use a question word such as *where*, *what*, or *who* to introduce *wh-* questions and *if* or *whether* to introduce *yes/no* questions.

Do you remember <u>when they bought the house</u>?

Do you know <u>if their house has a garden</u>?

G GRAMMAR Rewrite the direct questions as indirect questions for an Inuit hunter, starting with the words given.

1. Is it still possible to live from the land?

    Can you tell me if _____?

2. Have you lived here all your life?

    Can you tell me if _____?

3. How much has the animal population decreased in that time?

    Do you know how much _____?

4. How are you continuing your traditional way of life?

    Can you explain _____?

5. How big is the Inuit population nowadays?

    Do you know _____?

H GRAMMAR Complete this interview with an Inuit hunter by writing the questions in full. Then read the conversation with a partner.

A: What does the word *igloo* mean?

B: *Igloo* means "house" in Inuit languages.

A: Do traditional igloos [1]_____ _____?

B: They do still exist, but most people live in wooden houses now.

A: So can you explain when [2]_____ _____?

B: We use igloos for hunting trips—like a tent.

A: And can I ask [3]_____ _____

to build one?

B: It takes about an hour to build one.

A: That's fast. How many rooms [4]_____ _____?

B: A hunting igloo has just one room.

A: Did a family igloo [5]_____ _____?

B: No, it usually had three or four rooms.

A: And is [6]_____ _____?

B: No, actually it's very warm inside.

Baker Lake, Nunavut, Canada

REFLECT   Evaluate changes to your childhood home.

Work with a partner. Ask each other questions about changes to your childhood home. Use the ideas below. Ask both direct and indirect questions.

▸ Place of your childhood home
▸ Changes that have happened there
▸ Reasons for the changes
▸ What you think about these changes

PREPARE TO LISTEN

A PREVIEW Work with a partner. Look at the photos and describe what you see. What do you think might attract people to live in each place?

B VOCABULARY Listen to the words in bold. Match the questions with the answers. Work with a partner to discuss the meanings of the words. 🎧 1.4

1. _____ Do you live in the center of the city?

2. _____ Do you know when the town dates back to?

3. _____ Do you like the town where you work?

4. _____ Can I ask if your parents are happy living in Dubai?

5. _____ Did you fix that boat yourself?

6. _____ Are they building a traditional style house?

7. _____ Does the city have a lot of factories?

8. _____ Do you know why Robben Island is famous?

9. _____ What makes New Orleans different from other U.S. cities?

10. _____ Can you tell me what interests you about South America?

a. Oh, all **aspects**—the geography, the people, and the culture.

b. Because it's **associated with** Nelson Mandela, who was a prisoner there.

c. No, I have no **attachment** to it. It's just where the office is.

d. It's a city with a **distinctive** character all of its own.

e. It was founded in Roman times. It has great **historical** importance.

f. Yes, it's a very **industrial** city.

g. Yes. It's the most difficult thing I've ever fixed. I'm very **proud of** it.

h. Yes, they have a great **quality of life**—sun, exercise, good food, and friends.

i. No, I live in a **suburb** in the north.

j. Yes, they want it to fit in with its **surroundings**.

C PERSONALIZE Work with a partner. Write a place:

1. **associated with** a famous person _____

2. of **historical** interest _____

3. with a good **quality of life** _____

4. that has beautiful **surroundings** _____

5. that you are **proud of** _____

6. that has a **distinctive** character _____

Marrakech, Morocco

Hong Kong, China

Antigua, Guatemala

Alonissos, Greece

CRITICAL THINKING   Apply prior knowledge

When you are learning about a new topic, it's important to apply the knowledge and experience you already have. For example, when you think about what attracts a person to a particular place, consider your own experiences with various places and what aspects you find attractive. You can also use your knowledge of what makes each place unique.

REFLECT   Discuss connections to places.

You're going to hear an interview about why people feel attached to certain places. Think about why people form connections with the places they live. Use the categories below or ideas from your own experience. Take notes in the chart and then discuss your ideas with a partner.

Location	
Social life	
Work life	
Other	

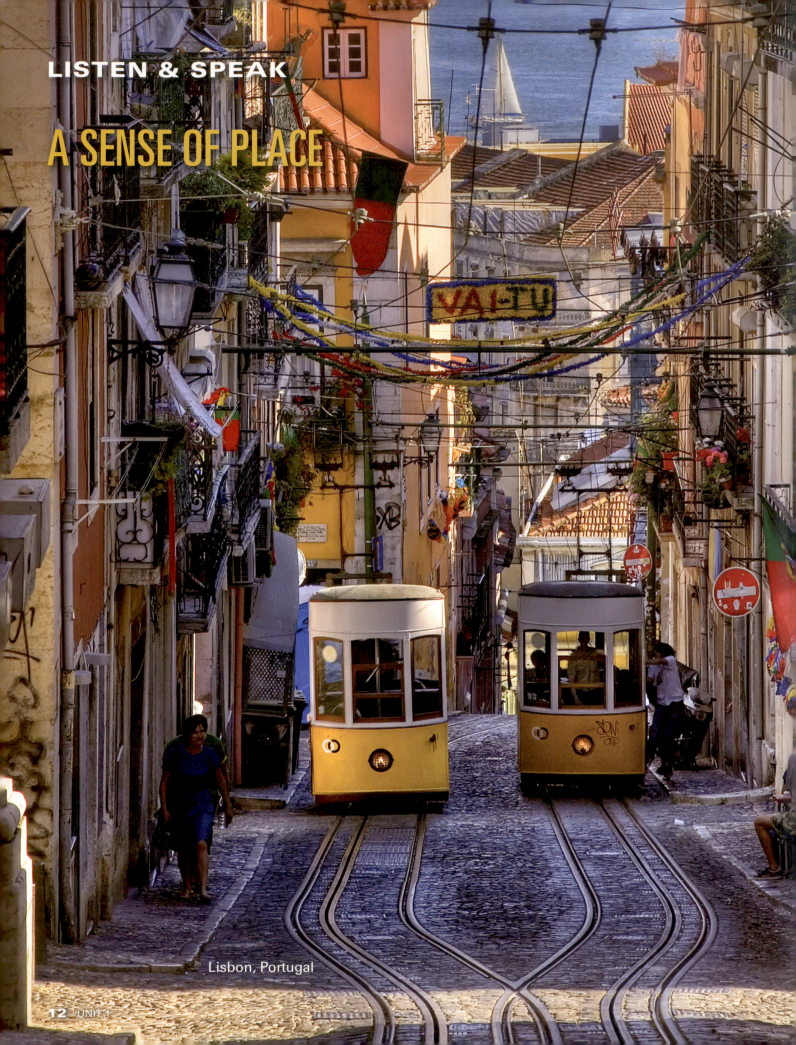

A SENSE OF PLACE

VAI-TU

Lisbon, Portugal

A PREDICT You will hear an interview between a geographer and a social scientist about what having "a sense of place" means. Tell a partner what you think it means.

B PHRASES TO KNOW Discuss the meaning of these phrases from the interview with a partner. Then take turns answering the questions.

1. How often do you **have your friends** over?

2. How is your **way of life** different from your parents' when they were your age?

3. What are some things your city or town **is defined by**?

4. What things do you **take pride in** doing?

C MAIN IDEAS Listen to the interview. Complete each sentence with no more than three words. 🎧 1.5

1. Place is more than just physical _____.

2. A sense of place is a person's _____ to a place.

3. Reasons for having a sense of place:

    a. The place has a _____.

    b. The place has a strong connection to _____.

    c. The place makes you feel _____.

    d. The place gives you a good _____.

D Work in small groups. How similar was the speaker's description of a sense of place to your answer in activity A?

NOTE-TAKING TIP

Follow these tips when you are taking notes.
- ▶ Note the main ideas.
- ▶ Only write down key words, but make sure you can understand your notes.
- ▶ Use abbreviations and symbols, for example "20th C" for *twentieth century*, "e.g.," for *for example*, and "%" for *percent*.

You hear: *In some cities in the United States of America, for example Jackson, more than 75 percent of the population has lived there all their lives.*

You write: *U.S. cities, e.g., Jackson, 75%+ of pop. always lived there*

E Listen to the first half of the interview again and complete the notes. Then compare your answers with a partner. 🎧 1.6

place = two things → physical surroundings

                        → ¹_____ of environment

place ≠ only areas of ²_____

place = people, ³_____, transportation, the ⁴_____

historical aspect also imp, e.g., cities = stops along first ⁵_____

F **DETAILS** Listen to the second half of the interview again, which gives the four reasons why we have a sense of place. Match each example given with one of the reasons. 🎧 1.7

1. _____ easy access to work   a. has a special quality

2. _____ the small village you live in   b. has a connection to your past

3. _____ your parents grew up there   c. makes you feel good or proud

4. _____ a beautiful part of the coast   d. has a good quality of life

5. _____ a friendly community

6. _____ an ancient university town

7. _____ your country

G Work with a partner to answer the questions.

1. Do you agree with the speaker about the reasons people feel a "sense of place"?

2. What are some other reasons that people can feel emotionally attached to a place?

A committee is researching what places are special to people and why. They have asked you to conduct interviews and have given you a short form to help you. You are going to interview another person in the class. Use the ideas, vocabulary, and skills from the unit.

H MODEL You will hear part of an interview. Listen and take notes in the form. 🎧 1.8

SPECIAL PLACE SURVEY	
Place?	Granada, in Nicaragua
Connection to place?	
Connection to past?	
Special qualities?	
Feeling of pride?	
Quality of life?	
Main reason it's special?	

Granada, Nicaragua

PRONUNCIATION   Reductions in questions 🎧 1.9

Words that help form questions (*do, did, have, can, could, would*) are usually unstressed. Sometimes, these words are also reduced. When we reduce a word, a sound might change or be dropped, or the word might combine with another word. Here are some common ways this happens in question forms.

Can you tell me what your connection is? /kɛnyuʷ/, /knyuʷ/
Do you feel proud to come from there? /dəyuʷ/, /dyuʷ/
Would you like more time to think? /wʊdyuʷ/, /wədʒuʷ/
What do you think about your city? /wɑdəyuʷ/, /wɑdəyə/

I   PRONUNCIATION Work with a partner. Take turns asking these questions. Then listen and check your pronunciation. 🎧 1.10

1.   Would you be able to answer a few questions?

2.   Can you explain why you like living here?

3.   Where do you go for vacation?

4.   What do you like to do there?

J   PRONUNCIATION Listen to these questions and write the question words. Then practice asking the questions. 🎧 1.11

1.   _____ tell me what kind of place it is?

2.   _____ parents still live there?

3.   _____ think of living in this area?

4.   _____ explain how it's changed?

SPEAKING SKILL   Check understanding and clarify

When you interview someone, it's important to make sure that they understand the questions. Otherwise, you may get the wrong information. Use questions and phrases such as these.

Questions to check understanding
Does that (all) make sense?
Is that clear?
Do you want me to go over that again?
Do you have any questions?

Rephrasing to clarify
I mean, . . .
What I mean (by that) is . . .
What I'm trying to say is . . .
In other words, . . .

Toronto, Canada, in the 1970s

Toronto, Canada, now

K APPLY Listen to excerpts from the interview in activity H again. Check (✓) the phrases in the Speaking Skill box that you hear. 🔊 1.12

L APPLY Work with a partner. Student A and student B each writes questions about their research topic. Take turns asking your research questions. Check that your partner understands. Clarify if necessary.

Research topic for student A: People's favorite vacation destinations

Question 1: _____

Question 2: _____

Question 3: _____

Research topic for student B: Places that have changed over the last 10 years

Question 1: _____

Question 2: _____

Question 3: _____

M PLAN Use the topics below as a guide for your questions about a special place. Write the questions you want to ask. Use direct and indirect questions.

Connection to place: _____

Connection to past: _____

Special qualities: _____

Feeling of pride: _____

Quality of life: _____

Main reason it's special: _____

N UNIT TASK Work with a partner. Take turns interviewing each other about a special place. Follow these steps:

▸ Conduct the interview, making sure your partner understands your questions.
▸ Note your partner's answers in the chart. You don't need to write an answer for each question.
▸ Tell your partner if they did a good job of checking understanding.
▸ In class, compare your findings. In what ways are the special places similar? Did people have similar reasons for their attachment to them?

SPECIAL PLACE SURVEY	
Place?	
Connection to place?	
Connection to past?	
Special qualities?	
Feeling of pride?	
Quality of life?	
Main reason it's special?	

REFLECT

A Check (✓) the Reflect activities you can do and the academic skills you can use.

☐ compare your home to someone else's ☐ notice tone of voice and attitude

☐ evaluate changes to your childhood home ☐ check understanding and clarify

☐ discuss connections to places ☐ direct and indirect questions

☐ interview someone about a place they belong ☐ apply prior knowledge

B Write the vocabulary words from the unit in the correct column. Add any other words that you learned. Circle words you still need to practice.

NOUN	VERB	ADJECTIVE	ADVERB & OTHER

C Reflect on the ideas in the unit as you answer these questions.

1. How will you think about places differently in the future?

_____

_____

2. What is the most important thing you learned in this unit?

_____

_____

UNIT

2 SOMETHING BORROWED

The "St John's View"
dining seatings upstairs

明爐燒鴨
水煮魚
麻婆豆腐飯
國水雞
豉味蝦仔飯
蠔豉瑤柱羹
干煸四季豆

Eat in or
Take Away

Cappucino
Smoothies
Hot &
Cold Food
Breakfast
Baguettes
Paninis
Wraps
Jacket
Potatoes

Cambridge, England

▶ CONNECT TO THE TOPIC

1. Look at the photo. What do you notice that is "borrowed" from another country?

2. What do you think *cultural borrowing* means?

21

PREPARE TO WATCH

A VOCABULARY Listen to the words. Complete the conversations with the correct form of the words. Then discuss with a partner what each word means. 🎧 2.1

admire (v)	debate (n)	meaning (n)	original (adj)	stereotype (n)
case (n)	influence (n)	offend (v)	particular (adj)	valuable (adj)

1. **A:** Does it _____ you when people don't say your name correctly?

   B: No, not at all. *Czeslaw* isn't an easy name to say. Also, there aren't many _____ of words beginning with *cz* in English.

2. **A:** You can't say all girls like the color pink. It's a _____.

   B: But *many* girls do. There's not a _____ about that, is there?

3. **A:** I'm just _____ your Turkish carpet. It's very beautiful. Is it worth a lot of money?

   B: No, but it's very _____ to *me* because my aunt gave it to me.

4. **A:** What's had the biggest _____ on the food you eat?

   B: Mmm, my mother's cooking has had a huge effect on me. She's from Italy, so when she cooks traditional Italian dishes, they have a special _____ for me.

5. **A:** I love that vase of yours. It looks very old, too.

   B: Oh, that. It's nice, isn't it? It's actually modern, but the _____ style is based on a(n) _____ 17th-century design.

B You will hear someone talking about one of her favorite things from another culture. Listen and complete the notes with the words. 🎧 2.2

American	*Avatar*	Japanese	*Pokémon*

Favorite thing: ¹_____ anime

Original films: *Akira*, ²_____, *Dragon Ball*

Anime is an influence on ³_____ films: ⁴_____, *The Lion King*

Son Goku from the
Dragon Ball series

C Listen again. Check (✓) the phrase from the Tip box that the speaker uses to check if the listener already knows about the subject she's discussing. 🎧 2.2

D PERSONALIZE Discuss the questions with a partner.

1. What parts of your culture are **valuable** to you?
2. What are some things that **offend** you?
3. Who or what has had a big **influence** on your life?
4. What is something you **admire** in another culture?
5. What food has a special **meaning** for you?

REFLECT   Consider cultural influences.

You will hear a talk about cultural borrowing. Discuss the questions in a small group.

1. Which cultures have had the biggest influence on the way of life in your country/region? In which areas (e.g., food, language, music)?
2. Do you think these influences are a good thing? Explain.

WATCH & SPEAK

IS CULTURAL BORROWING A GOOD THING?

A PREDICT The video you will watch is called *Is Cultural Borrowing a Good Thing?* Read the Listening Skill box. Which type of talk do you think this will be? Watch the introduction and check your prediction. ▶ 2.1

LISTENING SKILL   Organize notes by type of talk

When you listen to a talk, it's important to organize the ideas you hear. Some speakers explain the structure of their talk at the beginning. In these cases, you can use the speaker's structure as a framework for your notes. Use the structure to write headings or create a mind map.

Here are two common structures for a talk:

1. Problem-solution: background to the problem, previous solutions, new solution

2. Argument or opinion: background information, arguments for, arguments against, and a conclusion

---

B MAIN IDEAS Watch the video and complete the main ideas in the mind map. Do not add the examples yet. Then compare with a partner. ▶ 2.2

Background
Main idea: there is a lot of borrowing in the
1 _____ today
Example: _____
_____

Arguments for
Main idea: learning from others is a
2 _____ practice
Example: _____
_____

CULTURAL BORROWING

Arguments against
Main idea: borrowing can sometimes
3 _____ the original culture
Example: _____
_____
_____

Conclusion
Main idea: borrower should ask
4 _____ first
Example: _____
_____
_____

C DETAILS Watch the main part of the video again. Match the key points to the examples. ▶ 2.3

1. _____ Common examples of cultural borrowing
2. _____ Borrowing that doesn't cause offense
3. _____ Borrowing that has caused offense
4. _____ A case of borrowing that is debated

a. Native American headdresses
b. Traditional music, like blues music
c. The Italian pizza and the Inuit parka
d. The obelisk, sidewalk cafés, pizza, yoga

A woman wears a parka during Paris Fashion Week.

D DETAILS Work with a partner. Complete the questions a borrower should ask before using ideas from another culture. Then watch the last part of the video again and check your answers. ▶ 2.4

1. Am I helping to create a _____ image or stereotype of another culture?

2. Does this thing I am borrowing have a special spiritual or _____ meaning?

3. Could my use of it make its meaning less important or _____?

4. Am I making a _____ from this thing at someone else's expense, or will they also benefit?

E Use your answers from activities C and D to write examples in the mind map in activity B.

F List two or three things from other cultures that are popular in your country. Ask the four questions from activity D about these things and take notes. Then discuss with a partner if you think any of them are examples of inappropriate cultural borrowing.

_____

_____

_____

_____

GRAMMAR   Modals

Modals are placed before other verbs to add a meaning such as possibility, ability, or obligation. Some common modals are *can*, *could*, *may*, *might*, *should*, and *must*. The verb after the modal is always in the base form.

To talk about future possibility, use *may*, *might*, *could*.

> I **might go** there tomorrow.
> We **could arrive** early if you want, but they **may not be** ready for us.

(Note: We do not use *could not* to talk about the future.)

To talk about general possibility, use *can*.

> The winters **can be** very cold in Russia.

To talk about ability, use *can* and *could* (past).

> I **can see** long distances fine, but I **can't read** without glasses.

To talk about obligation, use *must*, *have to*, and *had to* (past).

> We **have to obey** the law.

To give advice or to recommend, use *should*.

> You **should try** the soup—it's delicious.

G GRAMMAR Choose the correct modal to complete these ideas from the video. Compare your answers with a partner and explain your choices.

1. Learning from others **may / should** be considered a healthy practice.

2. There are some cases where people borrow from another culture in a way that **must / could** offend that culture.

3. A sportswear company **must / had to** stop selling some women's clothes.

4. Some people say you **should / can** come from a particular culture, but you **can't / might not** own that culture.

5. These are questions that a borrower **may / can't** consider before they use another culture's idea.

6. **Could / Should** my use of the object make its meaning less important or valuable?

H GRAMMAR Complete the text with modals. There may be more than one possible answer.

John and Kate invited me to their costume party next week. So now I
¹_____ find a costume to wear. I ²_____
buy one, but they're very expensive. So, I think I ³_____ make
my own instead. One idea I had was to go as a French onion seller. I've already
got a string of onions. I thought I ⁴_____ make the rest of the
costume with a striped t-shirt and some blue pants. But then I wondered if it
⁵_____ offend someone. What do you think? I really don't think I
⁶_____ do anything that upsets people.

CRITICAL THINKING   Justify an opinion

It is often not enough just to give an opinion on a subject; you need to explain why you have arrived at that conclusion. Then people can see that your opinion is based on evidence or reasons. For example:

opinion	reason

I think we must listen to people who are offended because their feelings matter.

REFLECT   Assess cases of cultural borrowing.

With a partner, discuss whether you think the examples from the talk cross the line from borrowing (OK) into appropriation (not OK). Then form groups of four and present your ideas to each other. Give reasons for your opinions. Use modals in your explanation and justify your opinion.

▸ The use of a Native American headdress in a fashion show
▸ People who are not African Americans recording and selling blues music

PREPARE TO LISTEN

A PREVIEW Work with a partner. Look at the word cloud of borrowed words used in English. Which languages are they borrowed from? See how many you can guess. Check your answers at the end of the unit.

balaclava
pajamas siesta **piano**
burger **café**
delicatessen
typhoon **karaoke** **guru** **mosquito** **umbrella** **caravan**
sofa **croissant** **emoji**
tea

B VOCABULARY Listen to the words. Choose the correct word to complete each sentence. Then discuss with a partner what each word means. 🎧 2.3

| complicated (adj) | logical (adj) | pronounce (v) | similarly (adv) | translate (v) |
| expression (n) | predictable (adj) | replace (v) | suitable (adj) | version (n) |

1. Are there different **versions / expressions** of your language spoken by different groups and communities?

2. Is the grammar of your language **suitable / complicated**, or is it easy to learn?

3. Saying "I lucked out" to mean "I was lucky" doesn't seem **predictable / logical**. Are there examples in your language of things that don't seem to make sense?

4. What are the most difficult words to **replace / pronounce** in your language? In English, they're words with lots of consonants together, such as *strengths*.

5. What's your favorite **version / expression** in your language? In English, mine is "It's only money" because there are more important things in life.

6. Are there any cases where an English word has **replaced / translated** the word usually used in your language?

7. Do you sometimes find it difficult to think of a **suitable / logical** word or phrase to describe a feeling?

8. English spelling is not very **predictable / complicated**: you can't say how a word will be spelled just from hearing it. Is it the same in your language?

9. In French, all nouns are either masculine or feminine. **Logically / Similarly**, nouns in Italian always have a gender, too. What about in your language?

10. Can you think of a word in your language that you can't easily **replace / translate** into English?

C PERSONALIZE Work with a partner. Ask and answer six of the questions in activity B.

LEARNING TIP

When you study a topic, it's important to think deeply about it. Ask yourself questions such as these:

Is it really true that . . .?   *Could there be another reason for . . . ?*

Why? How did that happen?   *Who was impacted? How?*

If you can't find answers, then do some research. Ask someone you know, or look for answers on the Internet.

REFLECT   Discuss influences on languages.

You are going to hear a lecture about how languages influence each other. Discuss these questions with a partner.

1. What languages are similar to yours? How are they similar?

2. What languages have had an influence on your language?

3. How exactly have these languages influenced yours?

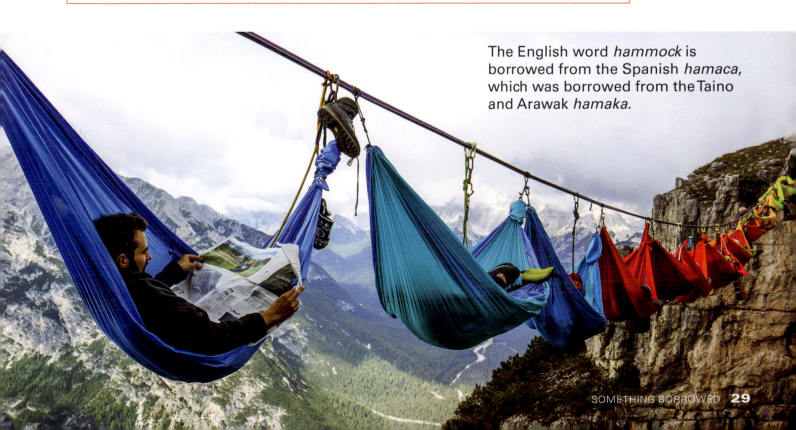

The English word *hammock* is borrowed from the Spanish *hamaca*, which was borrowed from the Taino and Arawak *hamaka*.

LISTEN & SPEAK

WORDS THAT TRAVEL

Women in the United Arab Emirates sing karaoke. The word *karaoke* is borrowed from Japanese.

A PREDICT You will listen to a lecture about how borrowing has influenced the development of languages. Choose the topics you expect to learn about.

a. Which major languages have influenced each other

b. The way languages take words from one another and change them

c. Why some languages are disappearing

d. The reasons that languages borrow words

e. How particular geographical or social groups contribute to language borrowing

B MAIN IDEAS Listen to the lecture and check your answers to activity A. Number the points you hear from activity A in the order you hear them. 🎧 2.4

a. __1__   b. _____   c. _____   d. _____   e. _____

C DETAILS Read the questions below. Then listen again and write the answers. Compare your answers with a partner. 🎧 2.4

1. Which major languages have influenced which other languages, according to the lecturer?

   _____

   _____

2. In which three areas can a dialect be different from the main language?

   _____

3. What is Australian English known for, according to the speaker?

   _____

4. What are two reasons given for one language borrowing a word or expression from another?

   _____

   _____

5. What does the expression *old timer* mean in German? In English?

   _____

6. What does the Korean word *dika* mean, and what is it an example of?

   _____

D PHRASES TO KNOW Work with a partner. Discuss the meaning of these phrases from the lecture. Then take turns answering the questions.

1. **On the one hand**, . . . we have cases of one major language influencing another.

   After **On the one hand**, how do we introduce a later sentence with a contrasting idea?

2. The reason they borrow the word is that there is no suitable word for that idea in their language. There isn't **an exact equivalent**.

   What words in your language don't have **an exact equivalent** in English?

E Complete this summary of the lecture using the words in the box. Then listen and check your answers. 🎧 **2.5**

| borrow | different | expressions | French | influence | original | Spanish | suitable |

Languages ¹_____ each other in different ways. Sometimes it's a major influence, like Arabic and ²_____. Sometimes it happens at the dialect level, as with Australian English and standard British English. Sometimes languages ³_____ words or ⁴_____ because they don't have a ⁵_____ word themselves, like the ⁶_____ expression *déjà vu*, which English has borrowed. At other times, they take a foreign word and use it in a ⁷_____ way than the way it is used in the ⁸_____ language.

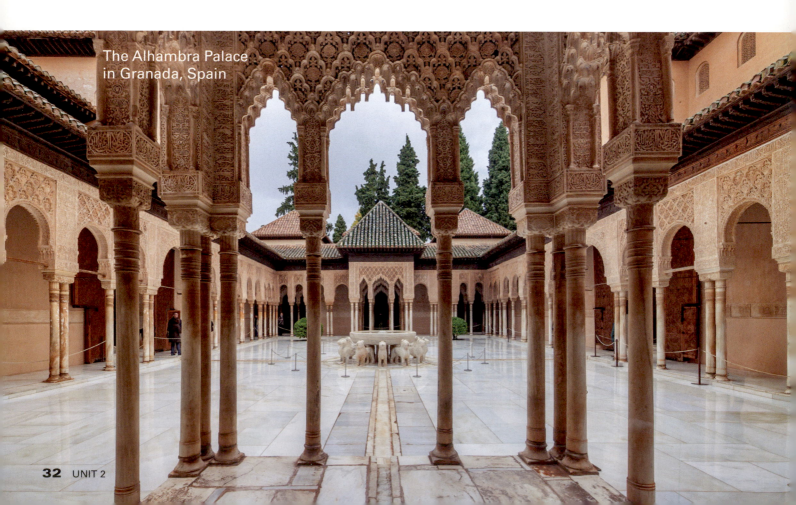

The Alhambra Palace in Granada, Spain

You are going to research words in your language that are borrowed from other languages. You will present your research findings—the borrowed words—with reasons why they have probably been borrowed. Use the ideas, vocabulary, and skills from the unit.

F   MODEL Listen to a presentation about universal words and what they have in common. Complete each statement with no more than five words. 🎧 2.6

1. Universal words are words that are _____.

2. Examples of universal words are _____.

3. French, Polish, and Chinese have a similar word for _____.

4. Universal words usually describe things that _____
    and are then exported around the world.

5. But not all things like this are universal words, for example, _____.

PRONUNCIATION   Consonant clusters containing -s 🎧 2.7

English has some combinations of consonants that can be difficult to pronounce, and many of these contain the sound /s/. These consonant clusters can be made of two, three, or more consonants together, and they appear:

▸ At the beginning of a word: **screen**
▸ In the middle of a word: i**nstr**uct
▸ At the end of a word: inter**ests**
▸ In more than one position: **str**en**gths**

Note that it's important to pronounce all the consonant sounds in each cluster.

G   PRONUNCIATION Underline the consonant clusters with -s. Then listen and repeat. 🎧 2.8

1. street
2. discover
3. describe
4. suggests
5. Spanish

6. worst
7. asks
8. months
9. thinks
10. translate

H PRONUNCIATION Work with a partner. Take turns saying one word in each pair for your partner to guess.

1. a. cream   b. scream
2. a. vests   b. vets
3. a. drink   b. drinks
4. a. worse   b. worst
5. a. masks   b. marks
6. a. retrain   b. restrain

I PRONUNCIATION Listen to the speaker and write the missing words. Then practice saying the passage with a partner. 🎧 2.9

¹_____, I'd just like to say ²_____ for the kind introduction. My talk ³_____ about 30 minutes, and then I'll answer your questions. I hope you don't mind if I talk from my ⁴_____.

SPEAKING SKILL   Report findings and conclusions

After you do research, you often need to report your findings and conclusions. You need to say:

▸ what you found
▸ what you are *sure* this tells you, and
▸ what it *may* tell you.

To do this, use these words and phrases:

> **I/We found** *several examples of . . .*
> **I/We (also) found that** *there were some differences.*
> **This shows us/It's clear that** *many words come from technology.*
> **This suggests/It seems that** *many words come from technology.*
> **Interestingly,/Surprisingly,/Not surprisingly,** *some are words for food.*

J APPLY Complete part of the presentation on universal words with words and phrases from the Speaking Skill box. Then listen to check your answers. 🎧 2.10

We ¹_____ these universal words: the words for *chocolate*, *metro*, *photo* or *photograph*, and *football*. *Chocolate*, for example, is very similar in many languages: *chocolat* in French, *czekolada* in Polish, and *qiǎo kè lì* in Chinese. We ²_____ that these universal words often describe things that start in or come from one place and are then exported around the world, like *football*. If this is true, ³_____ that most universal words describe recent discoveries. But, ⁴_____, not all things like this are universal words. The words for *airport* and *computer* are similar in some languages but different in many others. So, ⁵_____ that there must be other reasons for words being universal.

A photography class in São Paulo, Brazil

K APPLY Take turns reporting the findings and conclusions below to a partner in a similar way to the description in activity J. Use words and phrases from the Speaking Skill box.

Student A

Finding	Possible conclusion
French has its own words for most new technology, for example, *l'ordinateur portable* for the English word *laptop*.	French doesn't like borrowing English words (except for business).

Student B

Finding	Possible conclusion
English still borrows words from other languages to describe food.	Food is an important cultural influence.

L PLAN Find out about four words in your language that are borrowed from another language. Then follow these steps.

▸ Complete the chart for your words.
▸ Share your words with a partner.
▸ Notice and discuss any similarities you can find among your words.
▸ Then prepare to report your findings and conclusions about your words to the class.

Word	Which language is it from?	When was it introduced into your language?	Which field is it used in? (business, food, sports, etc.)	Why was it borrowed?

M PRACTICE With your partner, practice presenting your report. Ask your partner for feedback on your presentation.

N UNIT TASK Take turns reporting your findings and conclusions to the class. Then discuss any similarities among all the words as a class. Did anything surprise you?

Answers to Prepare to Listen, activity A

Arabic—caravan, sofa; Chinese—tea, typhoon; French—café, croissant; German—delicatessen, burger; Hindi/Punjabi—guru; Italian—piano, umbrella; Japanese—emoji, karaoke; Russian—balaclava; Spanish—mosquito, siesta; Urdu—pajamas

REFLECT

A Check (✓) the Reflect activities you can do and the academic skills you can use.

☐ consider cultural influences

☐ assess cases of cultural borrowing

☐ discuss influences on languages

☐ report on borrowed words in your language

☐ organize notes by type of talk

☐ report findings and conclusions

☐ modals

☐ justify an opinion

B Write the vocabulary words from the unit in the correct column. Add any other words that you learned. Circle words you still need to practice.

NOUN	VERB	ADJECTIVE	ADVERB & OTHER

C Reflect on the ideas in the unit as you answer these questions.

1. What are your ideas about cultural borrowing now?

_____

_____

2. What is the most important thing you learned in this unit?

_____

_____

THE LANGUAGE OF SYMBOLS

The Merlion is the national symbol of Singapore.

CONNECT TO THE TOPIC

1. What symbols do you see in the photo?

2. Why do we use symbols?

PREPARE TO WATCH

A VOCABULARY Listen to the words. Replace the words and phrases in parentheses with the correct form of a word in the box. Then discuss with a partner what each word means. 🔊 3.1

abstract (adj)	diagram (n)	exact (adj)	link (n)	significant (adj)
apart (adv)	document (v)	form (n)	represent (v)	symbol (n)

1. **A:** What's the _____ (connection) between a deer and a bull?

    B: They're both animals that people hunted in prehistoric times.

2. **A:** What information does that _____ (drawing) show?

    B: It's my family tree.

3. **A:** How _____ (important) was finding the dinosaur bone?

    B: It completely changed our idea about how big the dinosaur was.

4. **A:** What does the letter *H* _____ (mean) on this map?

    B: It's a hospital.

5. **A:** Were their findings _____ (written down)?

    B: No, they were never properly recorded.

6. **A:** Do you know the _____ (precise) date of the painting?

    B: No, but it's about 300 years old.

7. **A:** Are your earrings in the _____ (shape) of shells?

    B: Yes, seashells. Do you like them?

8. **A:** Does that tree on your ring mean something?

    B: Yes, it's a _____ (sign) of life and nature.

9. **A:** How far are the two sisters _____ (separated) in age?

    B: About 10 years.

10. **A:** Would you describe his painting of a horse as _____ (not close to real life)?

    B: Yes, I would. The artist is more interested in shapes and colors.

B PERSONALIZE Ask and answer the questions with a partner.

1. What do you think of **abstract** art?
2. What's one of your most **significant** achievements?
3. What are some common **symbols** people in your country would recognize?
4. How far **apart** are you in age from your best friend?
5. What kinds of things do people **document** in a diary?

Frieda and Diego Rivera by Frida Kahlo

C Listen to someone talk about *Frieda and Diego Rivera*. Discuss the questions with a partner. 🎧3.2

    1. Who is the painting of?

    2. What is the woman wearing?

    3. What does the bird represent?

    4. What does the painting suggest about the relationship?

D Listen to part of the description of the painting again and complete the paragraph. Use one or two words in each blank. 🎧3.3

He's in a suit and [1]_____ his paintbrushes. [2]_____ a bird [3]_____ over them—a dove, I think—which I suppose represents peace. But it's not a typical, happy wedding portrait. [4]_____ to be other messages in it.

REFLECT Describe artworks of historical importance.

You are going to watch a video about the significant discoveries of Genevieve von Petzinger, a paleoanthropologist (someone who studies the origins of humans using fossils and other artifacts), cave art researcher, and National Geographic Explorer. Think of a painting, sculpture, monument, or other piece of art that is important in your country's history. Then work in a small group. Describe your choice and:

▸ What it represents

▸ Why it is important

SYMBOLS IN EARLY CAVE ART

A MAIN IDEAS Watch the video. Take notes to answer the questions. Then compare your notes with a partner. ▶ 3.1

1. What did von Petzinger begin to look more closely at in 2013? _____

   _____

2. Where did she do her research? _____

   _____

3. What did she find there? _____

   _____

4. What did she conclude from this? _____

   _____

5. What idea was she also interested in? _____

   _____

6. What helped to confirm this conclusion? _____

   _____

Symbols from early cave art appear on a 16,000-year-old deer-tooth necklace.

LISTENING SKILL   Understand figures

Often in lectures and talks you will hear numbers or statistics. It's important to note what these mean because they are often evidence that supports the main argument. They may appear in the following ways.

- ▸ As a number: *8 years ago, 15,000-year-old, 6 million people*
- ▸ As a percentage or proportion: *30%, 3 out of 10, three-quarters*
- ▸ As a date: *in 2013, in the 18th century*

B APPLY Look at the notes. Then watch the video again and write the missing figures. ▶ 3.1

Chauvet cave paintings, France—approx. [1]_____ years old

Altamira cave paintings, Spain—approx. [2]_____ years old

Von Petzinger visited [3]_____ sites in total

Caves contained [4]_____ different signs

[5]_____% of the signs were the same

First writing systems appeared [6]_____ to [7]_____ years ago

Necklace with combinations of signs belonged to young woman who died

[8]_____ years ago

C DETAILS Complete the paragraph about von Petzinger's findings with the words below.

cave symbols	combinations	communicate	document	link	significant

Von Petzinger was the first person to ¹_____ the geometric signs in the caves. She realized that these signs represented ²_____ events in people's lives, which they wanted to ³_____ to others. Writing systems appeared later, and von Petzinger wondered if they had developed from the ⁴_____. Then she examined a 16,000-year-old necklace with ⁵_____ of signs like the ones in the caves, which seemed to show a ⁶_____ between the cave paintings and later writing systems.

D Work with a partner. Study the symbols from von Petzinger's findings and follow the steps.

1. Describe one of the symbols and say what you think it represents.
2. Discuss if you think there could be other explanations.
3. Present your ideas to the rest of the class.

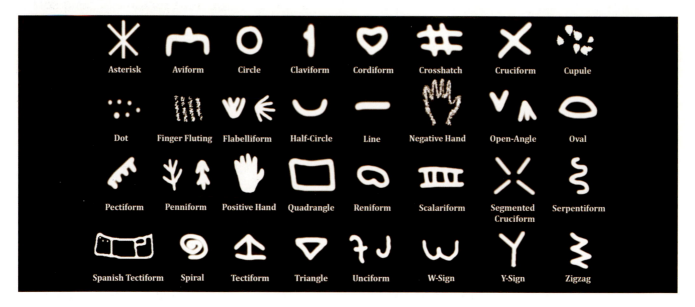

GRAMMAR   Past perfect

We use the simple past to describe past events as they happened, one after the other.

She traveled to Europe and visited ancient sites.

We use the past perfect (*had* + past participle) to refer to an event that happened before another event in the past.

*In May she <u>visited</u> the cave again and <u>documented</u> the symbols. But, as she <u>prepared</u> to leave, she <u>noticed</u> another small cave that she **had missed** on her first visit.*

We don't use the past perfect as often as the simple past, but we do often use it when reporting statements or thoughts.

*I thought you **had forgotten** about me.*

E GRAMMAR Choose the correct verb form to complete this account of von Petzinger's research. Then compare answers with a partner and explain your choices.

Other researchers [1]**noticed / had noticed** these geometric signs before von Petzinger visited the caves, but she [2]**was / had been** the first to document them. As she documented the symbols, she [3]**began / had begun** to notice a pattern. She found that 65 percent of the signs were the same, so she [4]**concluded / had concluded** that they were a kind of language for communication. Von Petzinger couldn't be sure that she [5]**found / had found** an example of early writing, but early writing didn't just appear. Clearly, it [6]**developed / had developed** from something that already existed.

F GRAMMAR Complete the text with the simple past or past perfect of the verbs in parentheses.

In December 2019, a team of archaeologists from Australia [1]_____ (publish) a description of an amazing discovery they [2]_____ (make) in a cave in Indonesia. The article in the journal *Nature* [3]_____ (describe) how they [4]_____ (find) the earliest example of cave art showing animals in the world—more than 43,000 years old. The archaeologists also [5]_____ (say) that the paintings represented a hunting scene and [6]_____ (be) the earliest example of paintings telling a story. Other scientists, however, [7]_____ (think) it was more probable that different cave painters [8]_____ (add) different paintings over time, making it seem like a hunting scene.

CRITICAL THINKING Make reasonable judgments

It is always best to make judgments based on facts. However, sometimes not all the facts are known or available to us. In this situation we must either:

▸ Recognize that we can't make a judgment, or
▸ Make a fair and reasonable judgment based on what we *do* know.

For example, you read, "Some people think the cave paintings of animals represent different positions of the stars at night." Your judgment: I need to see more proof of this BUT it seems probable that looking at the stars was an important activity for people in these times. At night, there was nothing else to look at.

REFLECT   Discuss the meaning of symbols.

Work in a small group to discuss the questions. Remember to make reasonable judgments and to explain your ideas.

1. Think about the animals in the cave paintings you heard about. Why do you think the cave painters chose these animals?
2. Now think of animals or plants that have special significance in your country or region. What are they, and what is their significance? Are they used as symbols anywhere?
3. Do any animals or plants have a special significance for *you*? Why?

PERPARE TO LISTEN

A PREVIEW Look at the symbols. Which ones do you use? How do you use them? Do you know where any of them come from originally? Discuss your answers with a partner.

B VOCABULARY Listen to the words. Complete the sentences with the correct form of the words. Then discuss with a partner what each word means. 🎧 3.4

| appropriate (adj) | come up with (v phr) | indicate (v) | species (n) | start out (v phr) |
| come across (v phr) | date back (v phr) | initials (n) | stand for (v phr) | universal (adj) |

1. It's not _____ to use emojis in a business email. Or do you disagree?

2. Do you know what the letters *LOL* _____?

3. Is nodding your head up and down a(n) _____ way of saying *yes*, or does it have a different meaning in some countries?

4. When you read messages with emojis in them, do you sometimes _____ symbols that you don't understand?

5. Are humans the only _____ that uses gestures to communicate?

6. Do you know who _____ the symbol for a heart? Because our hearts aren't really that shape, are they?

7. How far does the smiley face _____? Is it about 20 years old, or older?

8. What sign do you use to _____ that you're hungry? Can you show me?

9. They say it's possible that the dollar sign ($) _____ as the Spanish sign for *pesos*. Do you think that could be right?

10. When you write your _____, do you write the first letter of only your first and last names, or the first letter of any middle names, too?

C **PERSONALIZE** With a partner, take turns answering the questions in activity B.

D Match the verb phrases (v phr) in activity B to the definitions.

1. _____ : to find something by chance

2. _____ : to begin

3. _____ : to be from a particular time in the past

4. _____ : to think of or invent something

5. _____ : to be an abbreviation or symbol for something (e.g., *v* for *verb*)

REFLECT   Discuss symbols you use to communicate.

You will hear a lecture about some symbols we use to communicate. Work in a small group. Think about the emojis that you regularly use when you send text messages to friends. Then discuss the questions.

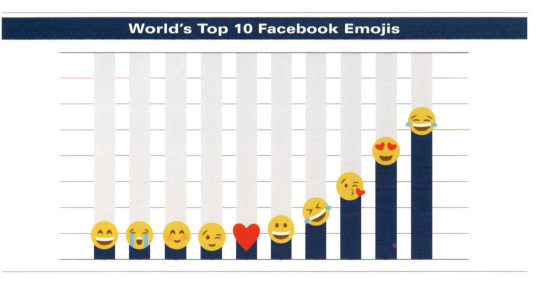

World's Top 10 Facebook Emojis

1. What do the emojis mean? Are they the same as the ones you use?

2. Do you find these emojis useful? For example, do they make your message clear, do they save time, or do they do something else? Compare your ideas with each other.

3. Is there a feeling or expression that you can never find the right emoji for?

4. Think of one or two other symbols that you use in texts. Where do you think they came from?

READ
THE SIGNS

A steep-slope warning sign, Torres del Paine National Park, Chile

A PREDICT Look at the photo and read the caption. Then answer the questions.

1. Is the meaning of the sign clear?
2. What is the connection between the photo and the title of the lecture?

B PREVIEW Listen to the introduction of the lecture and answer the questions. 3.5

1. What is the first point the lecturer makes about symbols?

   ____

2. He divides symbols into two groups. What are they?

   ____

   ____

3. Which type of symbol will be the focus of the talk?

   ____

C PHRASES TO KNOW Work with a partner. Discuss what the phrases in **bold** mean. Then ask each other the questions.

1. What traditions are **unique to** your family, as far as you know?
2. How did your country **come into being**? When did it become a country?

D MAIN IDEAS Listen to the rest of the lecture and complete the chart. 3.6

Symbol	Meaning	When it dates back to	Connection to meaning
✓			
@			

E Compare your chart with a partner. What does the lecturer say these examples show about symbols?

F DETAILS Read the questions below. Then listen to the lecture and answer the questions. 🎧 3.7

1. What did the speaker say each of these symbols indicated?

   a. a smiley face _____

   b. an arrow on a street sign _____

   c. a coat hanger _____

   d. a dot with three waves above it _____

2. In which countries does the check mark (✓) indicate a wrong answer?

   _____ and _____

3. What letter could the check mark represent, and what was its meaning?

   letter: _____ meaning: _____

4. What was the example of how merchants used the @ sign in the past?

   _____ @ _____ = _____

5. What two names did Ray Tomlinson want to connect in an address?

   _____ and _____

6. The Bluetooth symbol is made up of a king's two initials. What are they?

   _____ and _____

7. What was the king famous for?

   For uniting _____

8. What isn't important to know about symbols? What is important to know?

   Not important: where _____;

   important: what _____

G In pairs, take turns explaining the history of the @ sign and the Bluetooth symbol. Use the words in the box.

The @ sign		The Bluetooth symbol	
merchants	programmer	1996	united Denmark
cost	share information	3 technology companies	*H* and *B*
e and *a*	individual's name	connect wirelessly	dead tooth
each at	computer's name	Jim Kardach	blueberries
1970s		King Harald Bluetooth	

Design and present a new symbol.

There is a national competition for teams to design new symbols for different public signs. You decide to enter the competition with a friend. Use the ideas, vocabulary, and skills from the unit.

H Read the different types of messages that the organizers of the competition want people to consider. With a partner, discuss any signs or symbols that already exist for these.

    a.   A sign asking people to be more thoughtful toward other people in public spaces

    b.   A sign showing places where people can do particular activities

    c.   A sign asking people to respect the environment

    d.   A sign giving public health advice

I **MODEL** Listen to someone presenting a symbol they have created, using the visuals below. Answer the questions with a partner. 🎧 3.8

    1.   Which type of message in activity H is this symbol for?

    2.   Where does the presenter say this symbol would be useful?

    3.   Which of the three designs below is their final design?

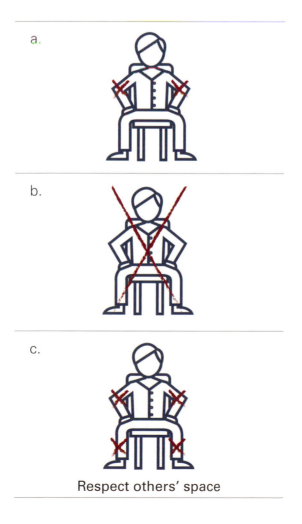

a.

b.

c.

Respect others' space

PRONUNCIATION   Commonly confused vowel sounds 🎧 3.9

English has more vowel sounds than most languages (15). Learning to pronounce them correctly is important to avoid misunderstandings. A common mistake is to make short sounds too long (e.g., saying *leave* for *live*) and long sounds too short (e.g., saying *pull* for *pool*). Short sounds take less time and involve less opening or widening of the mouth.

Short

/ɛ/ (pen)   /ʊ/ (pull)

/ɪ/ (live)   /ɑ/ (not)

Long

/eʸ/ (pain)   /uʷ/ (pool)

/iʸ/ (leave)   /oʷ/ (note)

Two commonly confused short sounds are:

/ʌ/ (luck)   /ɑ/ (lock)

J   PRONUNCIATION Look at the words below from the presentation you heard. Choose the words that have a long vowel sound. Then listen and repeat to check your answers. 🎧 3.10

1. sit
2. message
3. train
4. show
5. looked
6. seat
7. who
8. space
9. often
10. would

K   PRONUNCIATION For each word, match the vowel sounds in bold with a word in the Pronunciation box, for example, *sit—live*. Then practice saying the word pairs with a partner. Try to exaggerate the length of the long vowels and the shortness of the short vowels.

1. s**i**t _____live_____
2. m**e**ssage _____
3. tr**ai**n _____
4. sh**o**w _____
5. l**oo**ked _____
6. s**ea**t _____
7. wh**o** _____
8. sp**a**ce _____
9. **o**ften _____
10. w**ou**ld _____

L   PRONUNCIATION Listen to these sentences and underline the words you hear. Then practice saying them with the correct pronunciation. 🎧 3.11

1. Did you **test / taste** the cake while it was still hot?
2. Where did you **slip / sleep**—on the floor?
3. Excuse me, I didn't hear you. Did you say **shut / shot**?
4. Is there something wrong with your **foot / food**?
5. Could you pass me the **pepper / paper**, please?
6. We bought the baby a new **coat / cot**.

M APPLY Complete part of the presentation on a new symbol with words and phrases from the Speaking Skill box. Then listen to check your answers. 🎧 3.12

So, ¹_____ this first slide, our symbol indicates that the person should keep

their arms in. This next slide ²_____ an earlier version of the symbol we

worked on, but we decided that this was confusing: maybe people would think they couldn't sit here

at all. ³_____ the last slide, you can see we have another version.

N APPLY Imagine you are presenting this sign. With a partner, practice what you would say.

The Integratron in Landers, California, USA, offers sound baths for deep relaxation.

O PLAN Work with a partner. Choose two of the types of messages for the competition from activity H and follow the steps.

▶ Complete the chart.
▶ For the signs, describe or make a simple drawing of the symbol(s) you want to use and add any words you want to use.
▶ Create your final design to present to the class.

Message	Sign	Where useful	Meaning of symbol(s)

P PRACTICE With your partner, decide who will present each sign to the class and practice your presentations using your signs. Tell your partner if he or she referred to the visual clearly.

Q UNIT TASK Present your signs to the class. Then take a vote on which should go forward in the competition.

A sign reminds people to think of the environment in Somerset, South West England.

WHAT WOULD GRETA DO?

REFLECT

A Check (✓) the Reflect activities you can do and the academic skills you can use.

- ☐ describe artworks of historical importance
- ☐ discuss the meaning of symbols
- ☐ discuss symbols you use to communicate
- ☐ design and present a new symbol

- ☐ understand figures
- ☐ refer to visuals in a presentation
- ☐ past perfect
- ☐ make reasonable judgments

B Write the vocabulary words from the unit in the correct column. Add any other words that you learned. Circle words you still need to practice.

NOUN	VERB	ADJECTIVE	ADVERB & OTHER

C Reflect on the ideas in the unit as you answer these questions.

1. Why are symbols important?

   _____

   _____

2. What is the most important thing you learned in this unit?

   _____

   _____

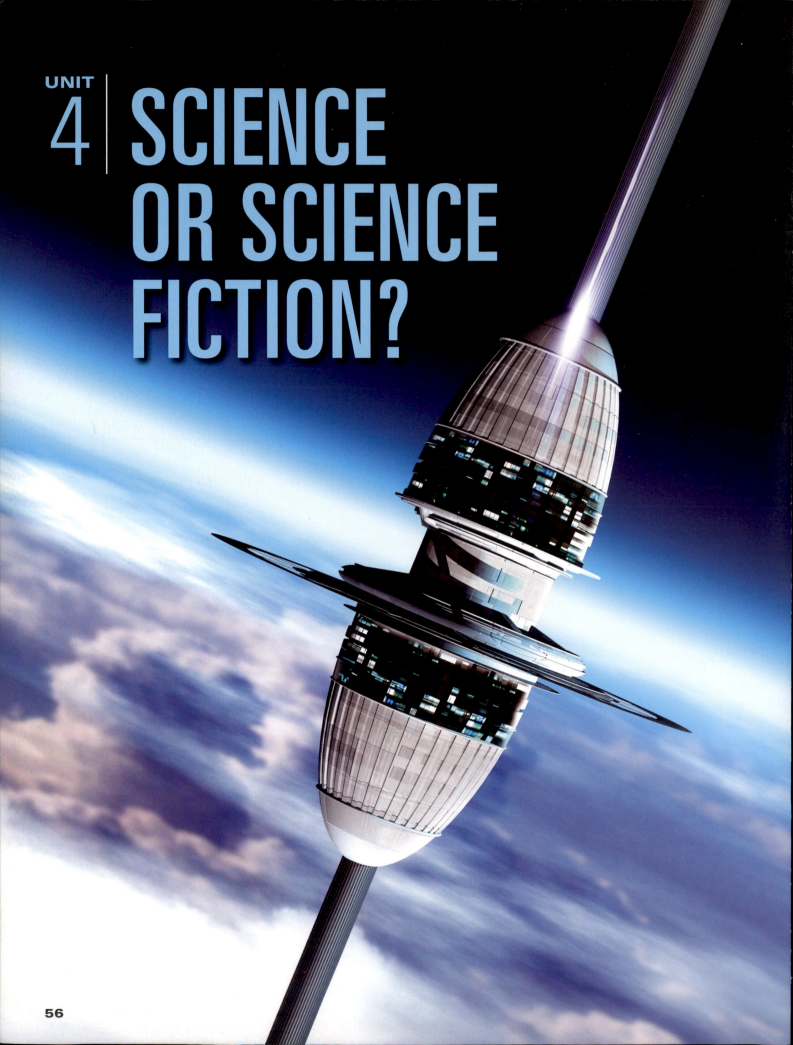

An illustration of a space elevator that could take people from Earth into space with the push of a button

CONNECT TO THE TOPIC

1. Do you think it's possible to build a space elevator? Is it a good idea?

2. Why is it hard to imagine what science will come up with next?

PREPARE TO LISTEN

A VOCABULARY Listen to the words. Complete the questions from a science quiz with the correct form of the words. Then discuss with a partner what each word means. 🎧 4.1

| breakthrough (n) | contribution (n) | detect (v) | | growth (n) | revolutionize (v) |
| characteristic (n) | curious (adj) | draw conclusions (v phr) | phenomenon (n) | specialize in (v phr) |

1. What do you call someone who _____ the study of stars and planets?

2. What plant has a _____ rate of up to 35 inches (or 89 centimeters) per day?

3. What Chinese invention of 8 BCE _____ human communication?

4. What unusual _____ does gold have?

5. What was Abu al-Qasim Al-Zahrawi's _____ to medical science in the 10th century?

6. What is the name of the natural _____ that causes objects to fall to the ground?

7. What natural disaster can a seismograph _____?

8. Which famous scientist said, "I have no special talent. I am only passionately _____"?

9. Archimedes got into his bath. How did this help him _____ about measuring the volume of objects?

10. What major scientific _____ did Copernicus make in 1543 after observing the sun and stars?

B In small groups, take turns asking and answering the questions in activity A. Then check your answers at the end of the unit. How many did you get right?

C You will hear someone answering survey questions about attitudes to science. Write her answers in the table. 🎧 4.2

Question	Answer
1. How much do you know about science?	
2. How do you feel about science?	
3. Is science or technology more important?	
4. Does science give you hope for the future?	
5. What problem do you want science to solve?	

In conversations or when answering questions, it's often necessary to indicate that something is your personal feeling or opinion, not what others generally think. To do this, use words and phrases such as:

As far as I'm concerned, *science is a bit scary.*

Technology is more important **for me**.

I'd say *science is more important.*

Personally, *I think we can be hopeful.*

D Listen to the interview again and check (✓) the phrases in the Tip box that the speaker uses in her answers. 🎧 4.2

E Work with a partner. Take turns asking and answering the questions in activity C.

REFLECT Discuss the role of science in our lives.

You're going to hear a science writer report on what future possibilities excite scientists. Consider your attitude toward science. Look at the information in the charts and share your answers to the questions with a partner. How do your responses compare to the statistics?

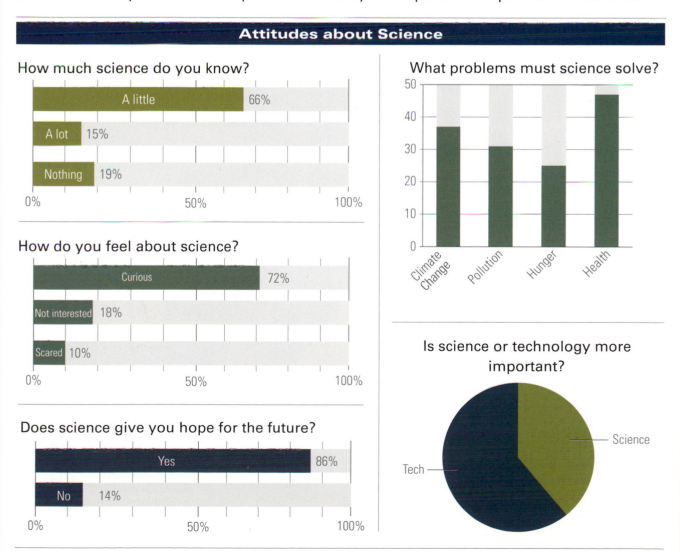

Attitudes about Science

How much science do you know?
- A little 66%
- A lot 15%
- Nothing 19%

How do you feel about science?
- Curious 72%
- Not interested 18%
- Scared 10%

Does science give you hope for the future?
- Yes 86%
- No 14%

What problems must science solve?
(Climate Change, Pollution, Hunger, Health)

Is science or technology more important?
- Science
- Tech

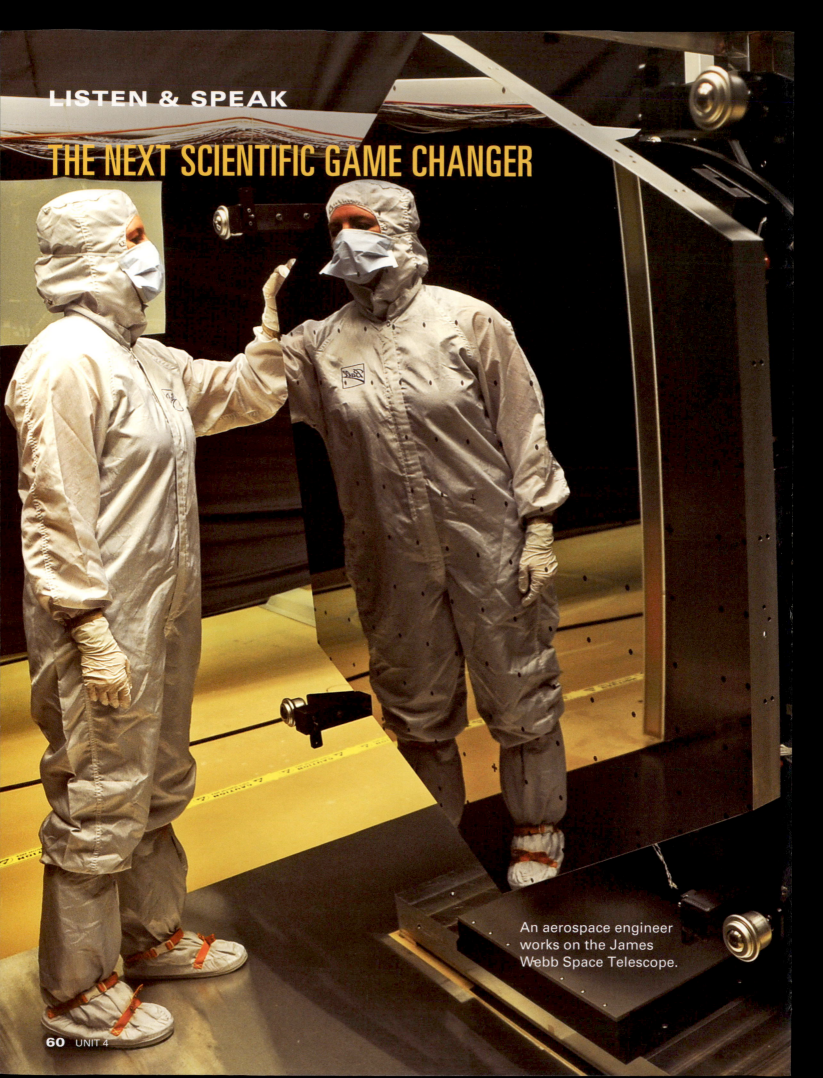

THE NEXT SCIENTIFIC GAME CHANGER

An aerospace engineer works on the James Webb Space Telescope.

A PREVIEW You will hear an interview about possible scientific breakthroughs in the next 10 years. Listen to the introduction and complete the sentences with a word or number. 🎧 4.3

1. _____ of people are curious about science.

2. _____ say science makes them hopeful about the future.

3. Fifty percent say science causes as many _____ as it solves.

4. People feel _____ that science can contribute to the field of medicine.

B MAIN IDEAS Listen to the interview. In which three areas of science does the expert talk about possible breakthroughs? What will allow these breakthroughs? 🎧 4.4

Area of science	Breakthrough(s)
1. _____	deep _____
2. _____	possibility of finding _____ _____
3. _____	universal _____

LISTENING SKILL   Recognize rhetorical questions

When you listen to a talk or interview, you may hear rhetorical questions. These aren't real questions because the speaker doesn't expect an answer. They're simply a way to make a statement more forceful and attract listeners' attention. For example:

Statement: *$100,000 is a lot of money for a domestic robot.*
Rhetorical question: *Who would pay $100,000 for a domestic robot?*

C APPLY Work with a partner. Choose the questions from the interview you think are rhetorical. Then listen to check your answers. 🎧 4.5

a. Who isn't interested in science?

b. What's "deep machine learning"?

c. Are there dangers associated with artificial intelligence?

d. How exciting would that be?

D DETAILS Read the statements. Listen again and write T for *True* or F for *False*. Then correct each false statement to make it true. 🎧 4.4

1. _____ The idea that artificial intelligence will change our lives is not new.

2. _____ Deep machine learning means that computers learn from the data they analyze.

3. _____ The speaker says that machines will use data to control weather events.

4. _____ One danger with artificial intelligence is the possibility that computers will use video or audio to show people doing things they didn't do.

5. _____ The new telescope means scientists can analyze planets in our solar system.

6. _____ The speaker is hopeful we will find a universal vaccine soon.

E NOTICE THE GRAMMAR Read the statements. Which describe things that are unreal in the present? Which describe things that are unreal in the past? Write Present for *Unreal Present* and Past for *Unreal Past*. With a partner, discuss which verb form is used for each.

1. _____ If fake videos became more widespread, we'd be in big trouble.

2. _____ If scientists had found life on other planets, they would not have kept it secret.

3. _____ If we'd had a universal vaccine in 2020, we could have saved a lot of lives.

4. _____ If I were a scientist, medicine would be the area of most interest to me.

GRAMMAR   Unreal conditionals

Conditionals are unreal if the situation is untrue, imaginary, or impossible, or if the situation was in the past and we can't change it. To talk about unreal events or situations and their possible consequences, use these forms.

Present/Future

I know nothing about science, so I can't help you.

> If I **knew** something about science, I **would help** you.
> *If + simple past,   would/might/could + base form*

I am not a scientist, so I can't help you.

> If I **were** a scientist, I **could** probably **help** you.

I can't get a new computer because I don't have enough money.

> I**'d buy** a new computer if I **had** enough money.

Notes: We use *were* for all persons in unreal conditionals. The *if* clause can come before or after the main clause.

Past

I didn't have any time, so I couldn't help you with your project.

> If I **had had** more time, I **could have helped** you with your project.
> *If + past perfect,   would/might/could have + past participle*

F GRAMMAR Complete the sentences with the correct form of the verbs.

1. If I _____ (have) the choice to live to 120,

    I _____ (not / take) it.

2. I _____ (go) back and meet my great-grandmother if

    I _____ (travel) back in time.

3. If I _____ (not / be) so bad at math when I was in school,

    I _____ (study) computer science.

4. If they _____ (discover) a way to grow meat before now,

    we _____ (use) more land for growing crops.

5. They _____ (solve) the problem of pollution tomorrow if they

    _____ (find) a new source of clean energy.

6. I had a parrot when I was young. If it _____ (be) able to speak, I

    _____ (ask) it how it felt about being in a cage.

REFLECT Imagine scientific possibilities.

Work with a small group. Which of the ideas are scientific possibilities, and which are only possibilities in science fiction (stories about imaginative and futuristic ideas)? Which would you most like to see?

- Reading another person's thoughts
- Communicating with animals
- Having constant clean energy
- Living to 120
- Growing meat in a laboratory
- Traveling in time
- Wearing exoskeleton suits
- Curing cancer

An exoskeleton suit, like the Hybrid Assistive Limb (HAL) worn by bus service employees in Tokyo, Japan, helps users do more physically.

PREPARE TO WATCH

A PREVIEW Look at the photo. When was it taken? What is the engineer showing and why? Share your ideas with the class.

B VOCABULARY Listen to the words. Complete the presentation of a new technology by a salesman with the correct form of the words. Then discuss with a partner what each word means. 🎧 4.6

bet (v)	dramatically (adv) *a lot*
commonplace (adj)	envision (v)
congratulate (v)	impractical (adj)
demonstration (n)	inspire (v)
device (n)	invention (n)

Hello everyone. Today I have for you a new ¹_____ that is going to change your lives ²_____. In a moment, I will give you a simple ³_____ of how it works. I ⁴_____ you'll want one when you've seen it working. Your friends will want one, too. In fact, very soon these will be ⁵_____ items in every kitchen.

We ⁶_____ a world where people don't use pots and pans anymore to heat things up. That is the old way, and it is a more ⁷_____ way, because it takes time and involves washing up. This ⁸_____ makes heating food simple. And I hope it will also ⁹_____ you to try cooking different things. Bring this home and your friends will ¹⁰_____ you on your smart purchase.

C The speaker is introducing a machine to customers in the 1970s. Can you guess what the machine is? Compare your answer with other students.

D PERSONALIZE Answer the questions with a partner.

1. Have you ever seen a **demonstration** of a new **device** in person or online? What was it?

2. What **invention** of the last few years has **dramatically** changed your life, or **inspired** you to do something?

3. What is a **device** that is supposed to help, but you find really **impractical**?

4. Do you **envision** technology making the future easier? Explain.

5. What is a new technology that is quickly becoming **commonplace**?

Sometimes you may want to talk about objects or ideas whose exact names you don't know. If this happens, you can describe the object/idea using different words and phrases, for example:

*There was **a kind of** flying car in the film.*

*I remember **a thing that** transported people in the film.*

*It **looked like** an old-fashioned telephone booth.*

REFLECT **Describe devices that appear in science fiction.**

You're going to watch a video about how science fiction inspired science. Consider devices you have seen in science fiction (sci-fi) films (e.g., a light saber or robotic hand in *Star Wars*). Think of one device to match each of the descriptions below. If you don't know their names, think about how you can describe them briefly. Then work with a partner to describe the devices and discuss why they fit.

▸ Something you found inspiring
▸ Something that has already become a reality
▸ Something that will definitely become a reality in the future

A British engineer demonstrates a newly-developed video recorder in December 1968.

WATCH & SPEAK

HOW SCIENCE FICTION BECAME REALITY

A PREDICT Look at the photo and read the caption. When did video chat became a reality?

B MAIN IDEAS Watch the video and match the points on the time line with the events. Then compare answers with a partner. ▶ 4.1

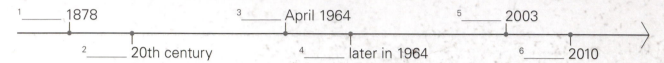

1_____ 1878		3_____ April 1964		5_____ 2003	
	2_____ 20th century		4_____ later in 1964		6_____ 2010

a. The first picturephone appeared at the World's Fair in New York.

b. Lady Bird Johnson made a picturephone call.

c. Apple Facetime was launched.

d. Skype was introduced.

e. The "telephonoscope" was imagined by a French illustrator.

f. Video phones appeared in sci-fi movies and TV.

C PHRASES TO KNOW Work with a partner. Ask and answer these questions using the phrases in **bold**.

1. As a student, would you be happy with only online learning, or would you prefer **face-to-face** contact?

2. Do you like to keep **a step ahead** of others when it comes to new technology, or is it not important to you?

3. If you could **achieve a dream** in the next five years, what would it be?

D DETAILS Read the questions below. Then watch the video again and choose the correct answers. Compare your answers with a partner. ▶ 4.1

1. What does a boss tell a factory worker via videophone in a sci-fi film of 1936?

    a. Get back to work!

    b. Stop smoking in the factory!

2. What do people like about the idea of videophones?

    a. Seeing people in color

    b. Face-to-face contact

3. The "telephonoscope" of 1878 looked like a combination of a videophone and what?

    a. A flat-screen TV

    b. An illustration

4. Where were the first picturephone booths?

    a. In eight American cities

    b. In three American cities

5. Why was the AT&T Bell Labs picturephone impractical?

    a. It was too big and heavy.

    b. It was very expensive to use.

6. Where did Lady Bird Johnson say youngsters would find the new invention a great joy?

    a. At college

    b. Traveling abroad

Two men using AT&T's Picturephone in 1964 in New York, New York, USA

E Complete the words of Lady Bird Johnson when she spoke to AT&T Bell Labs about their new picturephone.

bet	congratulate	grandmothers	joy	make	youngsters

"May I ¹_____ you and all who have helped ²_____ this

great scientific stride possible. I'm sure that there'll be many ³_____

off at college and many mothers and fathers back at home that will find this a great

⁴_____. I ⁵_____ your next best customers are

⁶_____."

CRITICAL THINKING   Summarize

Summarizing is one of the most important critical thinking skills in academic study. It is the ability to analyze a text, pick out the main ideas and important details, and then present them in a short form. For example, if you wanted to summarize the main idea of a science fiction film like *Star Wars*, you could say something like this.

It's a science fiction film about good forces trying to save the galaxy from evil forces.

You would *not* mention specific scenes, names of characters, popularity of the film, or other less important features.

F APPLY Summarize the origins of the videophone in a few sentences. Use the words and phrases to help you. Then compare summaries with a partner.

invention of telephone	expensive
first videophone 1960s	became commonplace with Internet

_____

_____

_____

_____

G Discuss the questions in a small group. Explain your answers.

1. What do you use video chat for?

2. Do you think the invention of video chat has improved communication?

3. What is one disadvantage of video chatting or video conferencing?

4. What do you think the next invention for communication will be?

Your college debating society has a monthly competition. This month it is to make a case for one of the most significant scientific or technological breakthroughs of the last 250 years. You are going to prepare a presentation for the competition. Use the ideas, vocabulary, and skills from the unit.

H MODEL Listen to a presentation on why reinforced concrete is one of the most significant scientific breakthroughs of recent times. Write three things this breakthrough has allowed people to do. 🎧 4.7

1. _____

2. _____

3. _____

I Answer the following questions. Then share your answers with a partner.

1. The speaker starts with "What would you say if I told you that reinforced concrete is one of the most significant scientific breakthroughs of the last 150 years? Probably you'd be surprised." Is this an effective way to start? Explain.

   _____

2. The speaker ends with "If it hadn't been invented, they would never have built the Burj Khalifa in Dubai or the Sydney Opera House." Is this an effective way to end the talk? Explain.

   _____

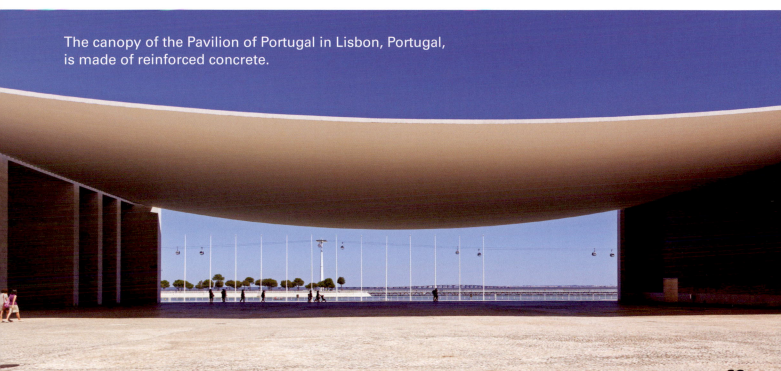

The canopy of the Pavilion of Portugal in Lisbon, Portugal, is made of reinforced concrete.

PRONUNCIATION   Rhythm and stress 🎧4.8

English is a stress-timed language with a regular rhythm. Equal time is spent on each stressed sound in a sentence. This means that, for example, *It's very strong* and *It's incredibly powerful* take roughly the same amount of time to say, even though the second sentence has more syllables.

The stresses are usually placed on the words that give the important information (the content words, which include adjectives, adverbs, nouns, and verbs) and on certain syllables within those words. The other words (structure words) are not usually stressed.

> It's in**cre**dibly strong, which means we can build **ve**ry tall **buil**dings in our **ci**ties.

J PRONUNCIATION Work with a partner. Underline the content words in this extract from the presentation. Then listen and double underline the stressed syllables in words with more than one syllable. 🎧4.9

But think about it. Reinforced concrete has allowed us to make buildings of many

different shapes and sizes. It has transformed our environment. . . . If it hadn't

been invented, they would never have built the Burj Khalifa in Dubai or the Sydney

Opera House.

K PRONUNCIATION Underline the stressed syllables in these sentences. Practice saying them with a partner. Then listen and check. 🎧4.10

Many people don't realize what an amazing material this concrete is. They think it's

ugly and functional. But it's changed the way we live and work completely. If this

material weren't available, the world would look very different today.

SPEAKING SKILL   Use rhetorical questions

One way of keeping your audience's attention is to use rhetorical questions. This means asking a question which you don't expect them to answer. Often, but not always, you will want to answer the question yourself.

> *What would you say if I told you that . . .?*
> *How could we live without . . .?*
> *So, what is the answer? Well, let me tell you . . .*
> *Where did the idea come from? In fact, it came from . . .*
> *Where did the virus come from? While we can't be certain, experts say . . .*

L APPLY With a partner, complete the rhetorical questions (RQ) used to express each idea. Then listen and compare your answers. Practice saying the questions. 🎧 4.11

1. Idea: 100 years ago, no one thought we could ever put a man on the moon.

    Rhetorical question: 100 years ago, _who thought we could ever put a man on the moon_? No one.

2. Idea: We couldn't manage without computers now.

    RQ: How _____?
    We have become so dependent on them.

3. Idea: Before refrigerators, people didn't have a way to keep food cold for long periods.

    RQ: Before refrigerators, how _____?
    The answer is they didn't. Refrigerators changed everything.

4. Idea: The telescope was invented much earlier than you think.

    RQ: When _____?
    It was actually at the beginning of the 17th century.

5. Idea: The reason most people don't believe the science is because they don't want to.

    RQ: Why _____?
    It's because they don't want to believe it.

6. Idea: Robots will replace most workers in the next 10 years.

    RQ: What would you _____?
    You probably wouldn't believe me.

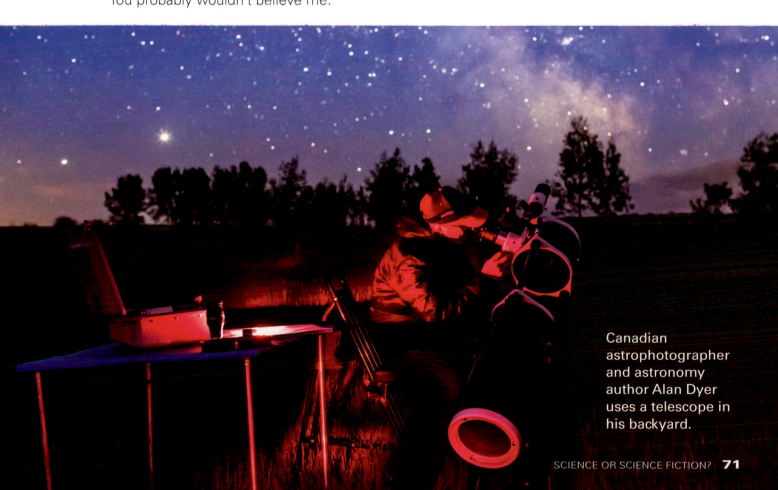

Canadian astrophotographer and astronomy author Alan Dyer uses a telescope in his backyard.

When you research a broad topic on the Internet, it can be helpful to be creative with your search terms. Use synonyms, specify dates (ranges), and narrow your search to a particular field or area. This will help you find information you otherwise may not have found.

For example, to research ideas for the most important scientific or technological breakthrough, your key words could be *interesting inventions*, *important breakthroughs*, and *breakthroughs of the 1900s*.

M BRAINSTORM Think about or research some scientific or technological breakthroughs and why they were so important. Take notes on what you find.

N PLAN Choose one of the breakthroughs that you brainstormed and researched and complete the chart below.

Breakthrough	When was it discovered?	Why was it important?

O PRACTICE Work with a partner. Present what you think is one of the most important scientific or technological breakthroughs. Use rhetorical questions and unreal conditionals to help make your case. Ask your partner for suggestions for making your presentation stronger.

P UNIT TASK Give your presentation to the class. Vote on which presentation was the most persuasive. What made it persuasive?

Answers to Prepare to Listen, activity B

1. An astronomer 2. Bamboo 3. Paper 4. It doesn't tarnish, i.e., lose its shine; it's soft; it doesn't rust. 5. He wrote a thirty-volume text on medicine and surgery; many consider him the father of modern surgery. 6. Gravity 7. An earthquake 8. Einstein 9. He noticed that the amount of water that spilled out of the bath was equal to the volume of the part of his body that was underwater. 10. That the sun was the center of the solar system, not Earth; Earth and the other planets orbit (move around) the sun

REFLECT

A Check (✓) the Reflect activities you can do and the academic skills you can use.

- ☐ discuss the role of science in our lives
- ☐ imagine scientific possibilities
- ☐ describe devices that appear in science fiction
- ☐ present a significant breakthrough

- ☐ recognize rhetorical questions
- ☐ use rhetorical questions
- ☐ unreal conditionals
- ☐ summarize

B Write the vocabulary words from the unit in the correct column. Add any other words that you learned. Circle words you still need to practice.

NOUN	VERB	ADJECTIVE	ADVERB & OTHER

C Reflect on the ideas in the unit as you answer these questions.

1. What do you think the next big scientific breakthrough will be?

   _____

   _____

2. What is the most important thing you learned in this unit?

   _____

   _____

THE PLASTIC AGE

More than 500 pieces of plastic found in the digestive tract of a baby bird in the North Pacific Gyre

CONNECT TO THE TOPIC

1. What items can you identify?

2. How much plastic trash do you think you could find around your neighborhood in one hour?

75

PREPARE TO LISTEN

A VOCABULARY Listen to the words. Complete the sentences with the correct form of the words. Then discuss with a partner what each word means. 🎧 5.1

addicted to (adj phr)	conscious of (adj phr)	invest in (v phr)	packaging (n)	urgent (adj)
be worth (v phr)	consumer (n)	material (n)	recycle (v)	waste (n)

1. Don't throw away your old phone. Take it to a phone store; they can _____ it.

2. Products we buy online always arrive with a lot of _____ around them.

3. _____ a metal water bottle—they aren't expensive—so you don't have to keep buying plastic bottles.

4. She realized she was _____ shopping because she felt she needed to buy things and then didn't use them.

5. Bamboo wood is an amazing _____. It's as strong as steel but much lighter.

6. Food _____ is a huge problem. In the United States, around 40 percent of the food people buy is thrown away.

7. I think everyone is more _____ the need to save energy these days.

8. The TV cost a lot of money, so it _____ repairing.

9. Climate change is a(n) _____ issue. If we don't deal with it, it will affect everyone.

10. The success of online shopping shows that _____ want the easiest possible way to buy things.

B PERSONALIZE Discuss these questions with a partner.

1. What **is worth** spending a lot of time on?

2. What do you think are good things to **invest in**?

3. What are some of the most **urgent** issues facing us today?

C Listen to someone talk about which everyday things in her life may contain plastic. Check (✓) the correct columns. 🎧 5.2

	Is mostly plastic	Contains some plastic	Possibly contains plastic	Contains no plastic
Breakfast cereal packaging				
Mobile phone				
Jeans				

Sometimes in discussions we are not certain or sure of our ideas. We can show uncertainty with words and phrases such as:

Perhaps the packaging contains plastic.

There is **probably** some plastic in it.

It could be that this is totally natural.

I imagine there's some plastic in this.

D Listen again and complete the paragraph with words or phrases that show uncertainty. 🎧 5.2

I realize there's ¹_____ plastic in all of them: there's some plastic

in the packaging around the cereal—though hopefully it's not in the cereal itself!

Then the phone's mostly plastic, and ²_____ there's some

kind of plastic in my jeans because they're stretchy. Can you recycle that kind of

material? ³_____ non-recyclable.

E Make a list of 10 things you use, wear, eat, or drink every day. Then write them in the correct box. Compare your results with a partner. Use phrases from the Communication Tip. Do any of the classifications surprise you?

Contains plastic	Possibly contains plastic	Doesn't contain plastic

REFLECT Evaluate the amount of plastic in our lives.

You're going to hear a radio program about plastic. Discuss the questions with a partner.

1. Why is plastic so commonly used?

2. Do you think you use more or less plastic than the average person?

3. What do you know about recycling plastic?

LISTEN & SPEAK

THE TRUTH ABOUT PLASTIC

A PREVIEW Listen to the first part of a radio program. Choose the main point the speaker is making.  5.3

a. Plastic waste is a problem.

b. Plastic lasts a long time.

c. Most things contain plastic.

B **MAIN IDEAS** Now listen to the whole radio program. Complete each statement with *one* word. 🎧 5.4

1. People have been very _____ in the way they use plastic.

2. Most plastic products are used _____ and then thrown away.

3. Only a small percentage of plastic has been _____.

4. The problem with recycling plastic is that often it isn't _____ doing.

5. We need industry and _____ to take more responsibility.

C **DETAILS** Complete the quiz with details that you remember from the radio program. Then listen again and check your answers. 🎧 5.4

QUIZ

FACTS ABOUT PLASTIC WASTE

A modern car is [1]_____ plastic.

[2]_____ of the material in our clothes is plastic.

Plastic lasts for [3]_____ years.

[4]_____ of all plastic becomes waste in less than a year.

Mass production of plastic started in the [5]_____.

Up to now, we have produced [6]_____ of plastic.

[7]_____ of plastic have become waste.

Only [8]_____ of the plastic produced has been recycled.

[9]_____ plastic waste goes to landfills.

[10]_____ of plastic waste ends up in the ocean.

Small pieces of plastic are in our water, the food we grow, and even in the

[11]_____.

D Discuss the questions with a partner.

1. Which fact do you think is the most significant? Why?

2. Which fact surprised you the most? Why?

E NOTICE THE GRAMMAR The passive voice is formed with (a modal +) a form of *be* + the past participle of the verb. Underline any passive verbs in these sentences. With a partner, discuss when you think we use the passive voice.

1. Plastic can be used to make many things: clothes, containers, and building materials.

2. We use plastic carelessly; half of it becomes waste in less than a year.

3. Some plastic waste has been burned, but most of it has been put into landfills.

4. In the past, we sent plastic for recycling to other countries, believing it would be turned into new products.

5. Many countries no longer want the rest of the world's plastic waste. They have enough of their own.

6. The problem of waste can't be solved by consumers on their own. Governments and industry must invest in ways to recycle more.

GRAMMAR The passive voice

Verbs in English can be active or passive voice. Active voice is more common.

> The world <u>produces</u> 300 million tons of plastic each year.

However, we use the passive when the person or thing doing the action (the agent) is unknown or unimportant.

> 300 million tons of plastic **are produced** each year.

The focus is on the amount of plastic produced and not on who produces it.

If we want to mention the agent in a passive sentence, we introduce it with *by*.

> Polystyrene plastic was discovered accidentally in 1839 **by a German pharmacist**.

The passive is an impersonal way of describing events. Therefore, it is common in formal and academic English.

> Recyclable forms of plastic **have been developed** to help reduce the waste problem.

Note: The form of *be* shows the time (present, past, etc.) in passive sentences.

Modals can also be used in the passive to express ability (*can, could*), advice (*should*), certainty (*will, would*), necessity (*must*), and possibility (*may, might, could*).

F GRAMMAR Underline the active or passive form to best complete the sentences. If both are acceptable, underline both.

1. **Someone invented the first plastic / The first plastic was invented** to make balls for games like billiards and pool.

2. People thought that if they could create a new material, like plastic, **they would protect natural resources, like trees / natural resources, like trees, would be protected**.

3. During World War II, **plastic provided a cheap alternative to traditional materials / a cheap alternative to traditional materials was provided by plastic**.

4. The environment became a political issue in the 1960s. That was when **we first observed plastic waste / plastic waste was first observed** in the oceans.

5. **Someone created the slogan *reduce, reuse, recycle* / The slogan *reduce, reuse, recycle* was created** in the 1970s.

6. Some plastics have very low recycling rates. For example, **you can't easily recycle plastic bags / plastic bags cannot be easily recycled**.

G GRAMMAR Discuss these questions about activity F with a partner.

1. Make *could create* in item 2 into a passive form. How does that affect the second half of the sentence?

2. How does the meaning of the second sentence in item 6 change when the active or passive voice is used?

H GRAMMAR Make active and/or passive sentences about ways to reduce plastic waste. Use the words in parentheses.

1. (supermarkets / do / more) Supermarkets could do a lot more to reduce waste. / A lot
   more could be done by supermarkets to reduce waste.

2. (pay / people / recycle) _____

3. (stores / not offer / plastic bags) _____

4. (the government / make / public announcements) _____

REFLECT Consider how plastic waste can be reduced.

What could be done by each of the groups to reduce plastic waste? Take some notes in the chart. Discuss your ideas with a small group and then present them to the class.

Consumers	
Industries/businesses	
Governments	

Sungai Besar, Malaysia

A VOCABULARY Listen to the words. Complete the sentences with the correct form of the words. Then discuss with a partner what each word means. 🎧 5.5

alternative (n)	concept (n)	long-lasting (adj)	manufacturer (n)	stuff (n)
by-product (n)	estimate (v)	make up (v phr)	melt (v)	trial (n)

1. One of the reasons there's so much plastic is that people buy a lot of _____.

2. Chinese students _____ 30 percent of the foreign student population at the university.

3. Recycling isn't a new _____. Two thousand years ago in China, people used old cloth to make paper.

4. Falling off my bicycle was painful, but thankfully I haven't had any _____ effects.

5. Many natural _____ come from cows that are raised for milk or meat, including leather for clothes, gelatin for candies, and fat for soap.

6. There'll be a _____ of the new computer system to make sure it's working properly before it goes live.

7. The buses are a quicker and cheaper _____ to driving cars in the city.

8. It was so hot this summer that even the roads started to _____.

9. I can't say exactly how many people were in the crowd, but I'd _____ around 20,000.

10. Some people say that _____ should be responsible for disposing of the products they make when people have finished using them.

B PERSONALIZE Which of the statements do you agree with? Discuss with a partner. Give examples from your own experience to support your view.

1. Too much **stuff** is thrown away these days. In the past, more **long-lasting** things were made.

2. I understand some climate change **concepts**, like the polar ice **melting**, but there are many others that I can't really explain.

3. There's so much money in coal, gas, and oil, and their **by-products**, like plastic, that business isn't interested in finding green **alternatives**.

4. History shows us that when a problem arises, people find a solution to it. I **estimate** in 30 years we'll have solutions to the problems of pollution and climate change.

REFLECT   Consider disadvantages to green solutions.

You are going to watch a video about a green technology. With environmental solutions, there are usually some disadvantages that need to be considered. Look at the green solutions shown in the photos. Work with a partner to discuss what disadvantages they could have.

Wind energy (instead of coal)

Organic farming (instead of using chemicals)

Electric cars (instead of gasoline)

Paper bags (instead of plastic)

RECYCLED ROADS

A PREVIEW Look at the photo. Discuss the questions with your class.

1. What materials go into making a road? What machines are used?

2. Can you guess how much it costs to build one mile (1.6 kilometers) of road?

3. How does road building affect the environment?

A road is paved with a special asphalt mixture in San Diego, California, USA.

B PREDICT Work with a partner. You will watch a video about a new green way to build roads. Discuss what possible materials are used to build these roads.

C MAIN IDEAS Watch the video and note the benefits and possible risks of this new way to build roads. ▶ 5.1

Benefits	Possible risks

D DETAILS Watch the video again and underline the correct facts. ▶ 5.1

1. The process uses plastic that would normally go to a **landfill / recycling center** and turns it into pellets, which are added to the asphalt mixture.
2. The plastic makes up **5 / 0.5** percent of the mixture.
3. The road looks like any other asphalt road, but it contains **6 / 16** tons of plastic in every mile.
4. The roads made with plastic are under **construction / trial** at the moment.
5. We don't know yet what types of plastic will be used or how easy the roads will be to **make / recycle**.
6. The manufacturers estimate that each square meter contains around **40 / 50** plastic bottles and 90 plastic **bags / types**.

E PHRASES TO KNOW Look at the phrases in bold and discuss their meaning with a partner. Then take turns asking and answering the questions.

In theory, the concept sounds like **a winner**. In practice, **time will tell**.

A lot of our customers have to be seen to be **doing their bit for** the environment and . . . this particular product . . . **ticks that** great big **box**.

1. Can you think of a product that's been **a winner**?
2. What **box** does it **tick** for customers?
3. Is it a product people will continue to want, or do you think only **time will tell**?

LISTENING SKILL   Recognize fact and opinion

When you listen to new ideas, it's important to identify *facts* and *opinions*. Facts can be proven. Opinions are what people think or believe about a topic.

Facts are usually just simple statements.

> The new system **is** 20 percent more efficient than the old one.
> The process **takes** several hours.

Opinions often contain a word or phrase that indicates that they are not factual, such as *I think*, *I believe*, *I hope*, *It seems (to me)*, and *Personally*. Adjectives that express judgment like *good*, *bad*, and *useful* may also indicate an opinion.

> **Hopefully**, this will be a more efficient system.
> **It seems** that the new technique will save money.
> The new roads are **better** than the old roads.

F APPLY Listen to some excerpts from the video and complete the statements. Then decide which statements are facts and which are opinions. Write F for *Fact* or O for *Opinion*. 🎧 5.6

1. _____ The plastic _____ into the finished road surface. It _____ around .5 percent of the mixture.

2. _____ The finished road _____ sheet of plastic.

3. _____ . . . _____ it will be more hard-working in the longer term and save councils money.

4. _____ _____ it's too early to say how environmentally friendly these roads are . . .

CRITICAL THINKING   Make a balanced judgment

A balanced judgment is one that is well informed and takes into account various perspectives. To make a balanced judgment when you read or hear about a new proposal or kind of technology, you should consider all the facts:

▸ what it does (its benefits);
▸ what it *doesn't* do (its limitations);
▸ what problems it raises (the risks).

By making a balanced judgment, you are better able to make the right decisions.

G APPLY Work with a partner. Summarize what you know about making roads with plastic: the benefits, the limitations, and the risks. Overall, do you think that it's a good way to recycle plastic? Explain.

Your school wants to raise money to sponsor a green idea for reducing plastic waste. You are going to give a short presentation with arguments for and against the idea. Use the ideas, vocabulary, and skills from the unit.

H MODEL Listen to someone presenting the arguments for and against turning plastic into oil and complete the notes. 🎧 5.7

Akinori Ito with his machine that turns plastic bags into oil

Advantages

Recycles plastic and returns it to its

[1]_____.

Oil has lots of [2]_____.

The process is quite [3]_____:

about 20 cents of [4]_____ produces

$1.20 worth of [5]_____.

Disadvantages

Machine needed to turn plastic into oil is expensive:

about [6]_____ dollars.

The oil creates [7]_____ when it

is burned.

The process doesn't make a [8]_____.

PRONUNCIATION   Stress in words with suffixes 🎧 5.8

It's important to put the stress on the correct syllable in a word. Incorrect stress can cause confusion for the listener, particularly in longer words.

In words with the suffixes *-er*, *-ment*, and *-able*, stress the same syllable that is stressed in the base word.

    con**sume** ➔ con**su**mer   **go**vern ➔ **go**vernment   re**cy**cle ➔ re**cy**clable

In words with the suffixes *-ion (-tion, -sion)*, *-ic*, *-ity*, and *-ial (-cial, -tial)*, stress the syllable before the suffix.

    pol**lu**tion   ener**get**ic   popu**lar**ity   fi**nan**cial

I PRONUNCIATION Listen to the words. Write them in the column that shows the correct stress. Then practice saying them with a partner. 🎧 5.9

| ability | activity | confusion | electric | reusable |
| acceptable | announcement | consumer | industrial | solution |

o O o	o O o o
_____	_____
_____	_____
_____	_____
_____	_____
_____	_____

J PRONUNCIATION Underline the syllables that you think are stressed in these words. Then listen and check. 🎧 5.10

1. ar•ti•fi•cial
2. ar•gu•ment
3. a•tten•tion
4. cool•er
5. judg•ment

6. or•gan•ic
7. pro•duc•tion
8. re•charge•able
9. re•spon•si•bil•ity
10. u•ni•ver•sity

K PRONUNCIATION Listen to someone talk about turning plastic back into oil. Write the missing words. Then read the text aloud to a partner. 🎧 5.11

I'd like to know what other ¹_____ uses there are for this oil. How will it benefit people? I'm not convinced that it's a ²_____ that's good for the ³_____.

SPEAKING SKILL   Present a balanced view

When presenting facts so that others can evaluate something, it's important to clearly indicate advantages and disadvantages. You can do this with words and phrases such as:

The main/big advantage of this is its cost.
Another/The other positive point is that it's very simple.
The main disadvantage/drawback of it is the possible by-products.
On the one hand, it's cheap, but *on the other (hand)*, it isn't very green.
Although the process is simple, it's very expensive.

L APPLY Use the phrases from the Speaking Skill box that you think best fit these statements about the plastic-to-oil idea. Then practice reading them aloud to a partner.

1. _____ the machine produces oil cheaply, it's expensive to buy.

2. _____ is that you don't end up with a green product.

3. _____ you recycle plastic, but _____ you still create pollution.

4. _____ is that it returns plastic to its original form.

5. _____ is that the oil has a lot of uses.

M APPLY Work with a partner. Each person chooses one of the green ideas below. Think about its advantages and disadvantages. Then present a balanced view of the idea to your partner.

Edible cutlery

This is the idea of an Indian businessperson, who was shocked by the amount of plastic cutlery (forks, spoons, and knives) used in the fast-food industry. He invented cutlery that's made from a kind of flour. The manufacturing process he developed uses 100 times less energy than plastic. After it's used, the cutlery can be eaten or safely thrown away. It can't be used more than once. The cutlery is quite cheap to buy, but it's still about twice the price of plastic.

Eco-cooler

First made in Bangladesh, Eco-cooler is an air conditioning system which doesn't use electricity. It's very simple: Small holes are cut in a board, and the necks of empty plastic bottles are stuck in the holes. The bottoms of the bottles are cut off, and the board is placed over an open window. Air from outside enters through the wide part of the bottle and comes into the room through the narrow part. In the right conditions—when the air outside is dry and moving—the air can be cooled by up to five degrees Celsius (up to nine degrees Fahrenheit). Eco-cooler can be produced very cheaply and is ideal for hot but not humid climates.

N PLAN Choose one of the green ideas from the list below or your own idea. Then complete the chart.

- ▸ Give students reusable metal water bottles.
- ▸ Grow a school garden.
- ▸ Compost (recycle) food waste.
- ▸ Go paperless.

Idea	Advantages	Disadvantages

O PRACTICE Work with a partner. Practice presenting a balanced view of the green idea you chose for your school.

P UNIT TASK Present your green idea to the class. Give your arguments for and against it and say whether you think it is a good idea or not. After you listen to all of your classmates present their ideas, choose the idea with the most benefits and fewest limitations.

High school students in Los Angeles, California, USA, turn garbage into soil to grow plants and vegetables.

REFLECT

A Check (✓) the Reflect activities you can do and the academic skills you can use.

- ☐ evaluate the amount of plastic in our lives
- ☐ consider how plastic waste can be reduced
- ☐ consider disadvantages to green solutions
- ☐ present arguments for and against a green idea

- ☐ recognize fact and opinion
- ☐ present a balanced view
- ☐ the passive voice
- ☐ make a balanced judgment

B Write the vocabulary words from the unit in the correct column. Add any other words that you learned. Circle words you still need to practice.

NOUN	VERB	ADJECTIVE	ADVERB & OTHER

C Reflect on the ideas in the unit as you answer these questions.

1. What is important to consider when you think about solutions to environmental problems?

2. What is the most important thing you learned in this unit?

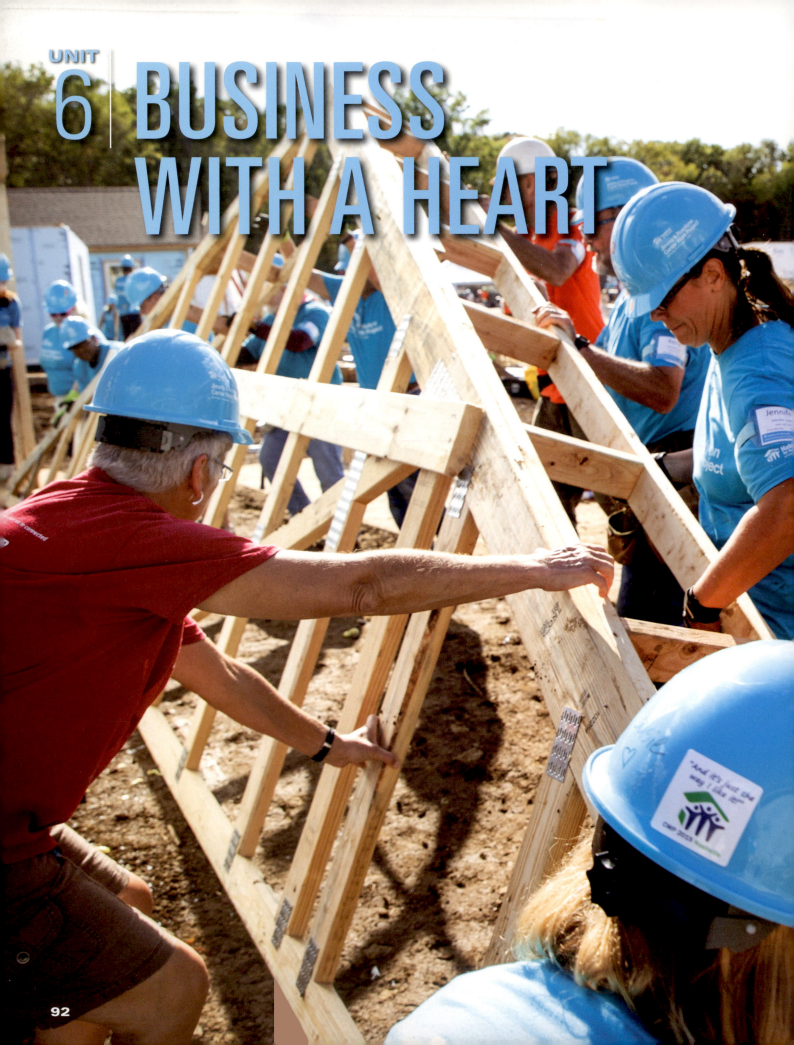

Volunteers work on a Habitat for Humanity construction project in Nashville, Tennessee, USA.

CONNECT TO THE TOPIC

1. Why do you think people volunteer for Habitat for Humanity? How do they benefit?

2. How can you support an organization like this?

PREPARE TO LISTEN

A ACTIVATE Listen to the phrases. They are all collocations related to the world of business. Work with a partner to discuss their meanings. 🎧 6.1

business model (n phr)	job prospect (n phr)	run a business (v phr)
customer loyalty (n phr)	make a profit (v phr)	volunteer work (n phr)
financially sustainable (adj phr)	market rate (n phr)	
have a mission (v phr)	raise awareness (v phr)	

B VOCABULARY Complete the questions with the correct form of the collocations from activity A.

1. If you bought a car from a friend, would you expect to pay less than the
   _____?

2. Does a business exist just to _____, or is money not the only thing?

3. Are a person's _____ better if they have a university degree?

4. Do you know what Facebook's _____ is? How do they make money?

5. Would you like to _____ of your own one day, or would you prefer to work for someone?

6. Sometimes in stores you find more shop assistants than customers. How is that
   _____?

7. Is doing _____ a good way to get work experience, or is it better to do a paid job?

8. Is advertising the only way for companies to _____ of their products?

9. Besides creating good products, what else increases _____ for a company?

10. Do you think every business should _____ to improve people's lives in some way?

C PERSONALIZE With a partner, take turns asking and answering the questions in activity B.

D Listen to someone describing a company whose products they use. Choose the things they mention. 🎧 6.2

Top reasons people stay loyal to a company

a. Product quality
b. Sustainable and fair practices
c. Brand name
d. Company mission

Top reasons people don't stay loyal

e. Poor quality
f. Bad customer service
g. Higher prices
h. Negative news stories/reviews

Our opinions about things often change over time. When we explain our opinions, we can indicate this using words and phrases such as:

I used to think that . . ., but nowadays . . .

In the past, I thought that . . ., but these days . . .

I've changed my mind about . . .

I don't agree with . . . anymore.

E Listen to the description from activity D again. Check (✓) any phrases in the Communication Tip that the speaker uses. Then compare answers with a partner. 🎧 6.2

F **PERSONALIZE** In your notebook, write the names of two companies whose products or services you have often used. Work with a small group to explain why you have or haven't stayed loyal to these companies.

REFLECT Consider how a company can affect people's lives.

You're going to listen to a lecture about what a social enterprise is. Work with a small group to discuss these questions.

1. Apart from customers, who else is affected by a company's activities?

2. What can companies do to have a positive social impact?

Bamboo Sushi is an environmentally sustainable restaurant in California, USA.

WHAT IS A SOCIAL ENTERPRISE?

A volunteer puts together a new bicycle for a child in need in Southfield, Michigan, USA.

LISTENING SKILL   Listen for definitions

In academic lectures, the speaker often explains key concepts that you may not be familiar with. It's important to note the names of these concepts and a definition of them. For example, you hear:

Brand loyalty is the positive feeling that consumers have for a particular product.

You write: *Brand loyalty = positive feeling for a product*

Listen for words and phrases that introduce definitions, such as *is, means, refers to, is defined as*, and *is used to describe*.

A APPLY You will hear the beginning of a lecture about the social enterprise model. Listen and complete the definitions. 🎧 6.3

A social enterprise = a ¹_____ that has a mission to cause positive ²_____ change and is also ³_____ sustainable

Support = ⁴_____ or ⁵_____ work

B MAIN IDEAS Listen to the complete lecture. What are the four different models of social enterprise the lecturer mentions? 🎧 6.4

To bring about social change, companies . . .

1. _____
2. _____
3. _____
4. _____

C DETAILS Listen again and complete the examples of social enterprises. 🎧 6.4

Example 1: An ¹_____ center where children can pay to paint a ²_____ ³_____ and gain ⁴_____ of the need for elephant conservation

Example 2: An ⁵_____ company that works with people who have a ⁶_____ finding employment, such as former ⁷_____

Example 3: A bicycle ⁸_____ run by ⁹_____ ¹⁰_____ that gives bicycles to people with no ¹¹_____

Example 4: A shoe company that promises for each pair of shoes it sells to a ¹²_____, it will donate a second pair to a ¹³_____ in need

D Rank the social enterprises in activity C by how successful you think they could be and how much social impact they could have. (1 = having the most success and social impact and 4 = having the least). Then discuss your rankings with a partner.

	How successful?	How much social impact?
Raising awareness about elephants through art	_____	_____
Finding jobs for people with few work skills	_____	_____
Donating bicycles to people with no transportation	_____	_____
Donating new shoes to children in need	_____	_____

GRAMMAR   Quantifiers

Quantifiers give information about amounts.

With **count nouns:** *(not) many, a few, very few, a number of, several, every, each, both, thousands of*

> *a number of* organizations, **both** businesses

We use *each* and *every* with a singular noun, and they require a singular verb.

> ***Each child paints*** *an elephant.*

With **noncount nouns:** *(not) much, a little, very little, a (large/small) amount of, a great deal of*

> *a little* information, **not much** money

We use *much* in questions and negative sentences but not usually in affirmative statements.

> *Does the company give* **much training**?
> *The company isn't making* **much money**.

With both **count** and **noncount nouns:** *all (the), a lot of, plenty of, most, some, no, none of the, (not) any*

> *a lot of* money and *a lot of* good ideas

Note that *a few* and *a little* = some; *(very) few* and *(very) little* = not enough

> *The business has* **a few** *volunteers but* **very little** *money.*

E GRAMMAR Underline the quantifier in each sentence. Then label the nouns following the quantifiers as SC for *Singular Count*, PC for *Plural Count*, and NC for *Noncount*.

These days, many young entrepreneurs prefer to start social enterprises rather than regular companies.

This is because they want to offer some help to others in society. Making a lot of money is less important

to them. So, we find that most social enterprises are not-for-profit companies. That means they don't have

any shareholders to pay, who only make money when the business makes money.

F GRAMMAR Choose the correct words to complete these statements based on the lecture.

1. **All / Every** businesses need to be financially sustainable.

2. **A little / Some** social enterprises rely on the profits generated by the business in order to survive.

3. **Many / Much** others require extra support, such as donations or volunteer work.

4. The employment company gives **a lot of / much** support to the job seekers.

5. The company benefits by making **many / much** more job placements.

6. The job seekers benefit because they gain **several / some** valuable experience.

7. Old bicycles are repaired and given to local people who have **any / no** transportation.

8. For **all / every** pair of shoes it sells, TOMS gives a second pair to a child in need.

9. **A few / A little** social enterprises follow just one business model.

10. But **most / a great deal of** social enterprises combine more than one model in their business.

REFLECT   Analyze data about social enterprise.

Work with a partner. Look at the infographic. Then read the sentences to each other, replacing the percentages with quantifiers. Discuss what the statistics tell you.

Some of the world's social entrepreneurs have had financial help from their family. Maybe they used the money to start their businesses.

Social Enterprise Facts

24% of the world's social entrepreneurs have had financial help from their family.

38% of the world's social enterprises receive government funding.

5.75% of the U.S. population is involved with a social enterprise in some way.

44% of the world's social enterprises are run by women.

78% of U.K. social enterprises have no employees.

Only **16.5%** of social enterprises in Mexico are still going after four years.

PREPARE TO WATCH

A VOCABULARY Listen to the words in **bold**. Read the interview. Work with a partner to discuss what each word means. Then choose the best definition for each word. 🎧6.5

A: For people with certain disabilities, having a regular full-time job is not really ¹**viable**. So, what are the main ²**barriers** preventing these people from being fully independent members of the workforce?

B: The main one is lack of access to buildings and to public transportation. We must ³**provide** the right facilities to ⁴**enable** these people to participate. Simple changes to signs and elevators can completely ⁵**transform** their lives.

A: But that can be expensive. Those things aren't always ⁶**affordable** for small businesses, which already have high costs compared to their ⁷**income.**

B: Yes, that's true. That's why the government needs to ⁸**identify** the businesses that need financial help and give it to them. It's the government's responsibility to help everyone in society to work and be ⁹**productive**. Small businesses shouldn't have to rely on ¹⁰**charity** from nongovernmental organizations to pay for these things.

		a.	b.
1.	**viable** (adj)	a. thinkable	b. possible
2.	**barrier** (n)	a. opportunity	b. difficulty
3.	**provide** (v)	a. make available	b. sell
4.	**enable** (v)	a. allow	b. force
5.	**transform** (v)	a. damage	b. change
6.	**affordable** (adj)	a. at a price you can pay	b. practical
7.	**income** (n)	a. money earned	b. money borrowed
8.	**identify** (v)	a. find	b. collect
9.	**productive** (adj)	a. creative	b. doing a lot
10.	**charity** (n)	a. agreement	b. donations

B PERSONALIZE Complete the statements. Then share your answers with a partner.

1. If donating a lot of money were a **viable** option for me, I would give it to

   _____.

2. _____ will **enable** me to better reach my goals.

3. My most **productive** time of day is _____.

4. _____ is the most **affordable** place to live in my country/city.

5. The main **barriers** to learning English are _____

   _____.

C Think about public places that you visit (schools, movie theaters, stores, gyms, etc.). What facilities do they have for people who have difficulties with their vision, hearing, or mobility? Are there any places that do not provide facilities for these people?

CRITICAL THINKING   Interpret statistics

Statistics represent facts. But you still need to think about the real meaning of these facts and what other information is needed to get a complete picture. For example, look at this statistic:

47 percent of disabled people aged 15–64 in the European Union (EU) are employed.

This figure may seem low, but we don't know how many people *without* a disability have a job, or if the figure varies from country to country in the EU.

REFLECT   Interpret statistics about disabilities.

You are going to watch a video about an entrepreneur whose goal is to help people with a disability. Work with a small group. Look at the infographic. Then discuss the questions.

1. Do you think these disabilities are different according to geographical location, age group, gender, and income group?

2. Is there information missing that could help you to interpret these statistics?

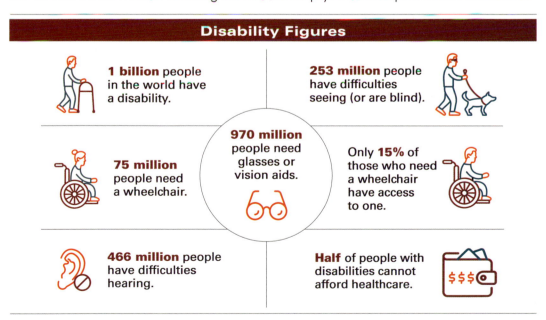

Disability Figures

1 billion people in the world have a disability.

253 million people have difficulties seeing (or are blind).

970 million people need glasses or vision aids.

75 million people need a wheelchair.

Only **15%** of those who need a wheelchair have access to one.

466 million people have difficulties hearing.

Half of people with disabilities cannot afford healthcare.

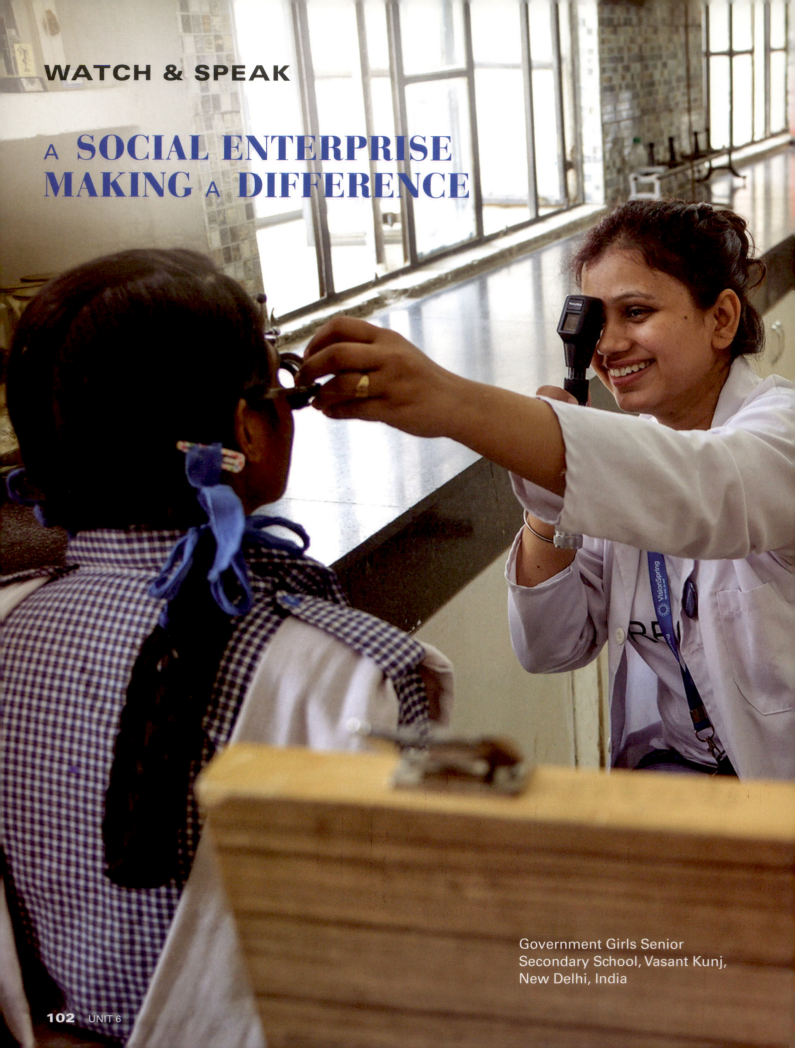

A SOCIAL ENTERPRISE MAKING A DIFFERENCE

Government Girls Senior
Secondary School, Vasant Kunj,
New Delhi, India

A PREDICT Look at the photo. What do you think the social enterprise in the video does?

B MAIN IDEAS Read these questions about the social enterprise VisionSpring. Watch the video. Then discuss the answers with a partner. ▶ 6.1

1. What products and services does it provide?
2. Who delivers these services?
3. How does VisionSpring manage to be financially sustainable?

C PHRASES TO KNOW Work with a partner. Look at the phrases from the video. Then complete the questions in your own words. Take turns asking and answering the questions.

1. Not everyone can **point to a moment** in time that transformed their lives . . .
   Can you **point to a moment** that _____?

2. . . . we're not going to **make a** big enough **dent in** the overall problem.
   How can we **make a dent in** the problem of _____?

3. . . . we source glasses as low as we can **in terms of** price points.
   Do you think our school is good **in terms of** _____?

D DETAILS Watch the video again and complete the notes. ▶ 6.1

Jordan Kassalow's background	Trained as an [1]_____
Moment that transformed his life	Put glasses on a boy who people thought was [2]_____
Reason vision is important	Enables us to [3]_____ others and to be [4]_____
What most people need	[5]_____ eyeglasses
What Vision Entrepreneurs do	Go [6]_____ educating people about the need for better vision and referring people who need [7]_____
Business model	Buy glasses at a low [8]_____ and sell them for a little more
VisionSpring's mission	To create a world where vision is not a barrier to [9]_____ development

E DETAILS Match the facts with the figures. Then watch part of the video again to check your answers. ▶ 6.2

1. _____ Number of people needing glasses who don't have access to affordable glasses
2. _____ Amount of the population that needs simple supermarket-style eyeglasses
3. _____ Daily income needed to afford VisionSpring glasses
4. _____ Number of VisionSpring customers annually
5. _____ Amount these productive customers add to the economy

a. Two-thirds
b. 1 million
c. $756 million
d. 95 percent
e. $1–$4

F Work with a small group. Discuss the questions.

1. What social enterprise model (or models) does VisionSpring follow?
2. What are the good points about it? Make a list.
3. Can you see any problems or risks with it?

Eyeglasses for sale

Your community is looking for good ideas for a social enterprise to help people in need (e.g., with food, education, social care). You are going to present your idea with a partner. You will need to explain any new concepts in your presentation. Use the ideas, vocabulary, and skills from the unit.

G   MODEL Listen to a short presentation of an idea for a social enterprise. Then discuss the questions with a partner. 🎧 6.6

1. How can you summarize the idea for a social enterprise in a sentence or two?

2. What is the three-word term the presenter uses and explains at the end?

3. What other advantages to this enterprise can you think of?

4. Would you volunteer to look after a school garden?

H Listen to the presentation again and choose the correct answers. 🎧 6.6

1. The students **will / won't** be paid to look after the gardens.

2. The students **will / won't** gain work experience.

3. The social enterprise will be a **non-profit / low-profit** business.

4. Any money they earn will go **back into the business / to the cafeteria**.

5. The social benefit is that the students will gain **experience / friends**.

6. The environmental benefit is that there will be **more green space / less food waste**.

7. The main financial benefit is to **the college / the business**.

8. The social enterprise **passes / does not pass** the Triple Bottom Line test.

PRONUNCIATION   Linking between vowel sounds 🎧 6.7

When one word ends in a consonant sound and the next begins with a vowel sound, the two sounds are linked.

   *I li**ve in I**taly.*

When one word ends with a vowel sound and the next begins with a vowel sound, we need an extra consonant sound to link the two words.

Words ending in /ɪʸ/ and /aʸ/ are linked to the next word with a *y* sound.

   He ʸis an entrepreneur.

Words ending in /uʷ/ and /oʷ/ are linked to the next word with a *w* sound.

   *Go t**o ʷa** bank.*

I PRONUNCIATION Link sounds in the sentences. Add a *y* or *w* sound where needed. Then listen and repeat. 🎧 6.8

1. Our idea is to turn a small section of the college sports fields into a vegetable garden.

2. We are a team of college students who are trying to promote social enterprise.

3. Our aim is to open up access to education.

4. They rely on donations from two organizations located in the area.

5. Would you be interested in donating to our organization?

6. Jordan Kassalow is a social entrepreneur and an eye doctor.

J PRONUNCIATION Work with a partner. Link sounds in the conversation. Then read the conversation with the linked sounds. Listen to compare your pronunciation. 🎧 6.9

A: How do you explain the term *Angel Investor*?

B: It's a person who invests in social enterprises.

A: Do they share in the profits of the enterprise, too?

B: Yes, often. But sometimes they do it just because they like the idea.

SPEAKING SKILL   **Define and explain a concept**

Often in academic study or work we have to define and explain specific terms and concepts. One common way of doing this is giving information with adjective clauses:

Triple Bottom Line is a tool **that measures three aspects of a business.**

The cafeteria is a place **where students can get affordable meals.**

We can give definitions in other ways too, such as:

Low profit here **is defined as** *less than 10 percent profit.*

This means *that they will sell vegetables to the college at a low price.*

This is called *the Triple Bottom Line test.*

K APPLY Listen to Jordan Kassalow's description of the concept behind VisionSpring. Complete the sentences with the correct words. Then underline the adjective clauses. 🎧 6.10

The world that I'm trying to create is a world where no ¹_____ falls out of

school because he or she can't see. A world where no ²_____ falls out of the

workplace because he or she can't see. A world where ³_____ is no longer a

barrier to personal and economic development.

L APPLY Work with a partner and complete the definitions.

1. A *social enterprise* is a business that _____.

2. *Support* in terms of social enterprise means _____.

3. A *volunteer* is a person who _____.

4. *Affordable* is defined as _____.

5. *Economically viable* means _____.

6. *To raise awareness* means _____.

7. *To make a dent in* means _____.

8. *Vision Entrepreneurs* are people who _____.

9. *Productive* here means _____.

10. The *one-for-one business model* is defined as _____.

A café in Istanbul, Turkey, employs people with Down syndrome and helps them gain self-confidence in business and social life.

M PLAN Work with a partner to discuss the questions about your idea for a social enterprise. Use your answers in your presentation.

1. What group of people do you want to help?

2. What product or service will you sell to help them?

3. Which business model will you use?

   Pay It Forward: Charge more than the market rate for a product and use the extra money for your cause.

   One-for-one: Donate one item to your cause for every one item you sell.

   Co-op: Form a group to run and benefit from a business.

4. What will you call your social enterprise and how will you promote it?

5. What advantages and disadvantages can you see with your idea?

N PRACTICE Decide how to divide up the information in the presentation, and then practice presenting your social enterprise. Remember to define or explain any new concepts.

O UNIT TASK Present your idea for a social enterprise to the class. What are the advantages and disadvantages of each concept? Which students' social enterprise ideas would work well? Which would you support?

For every dessert Michael Platt of Michaels Desserts sells, he donates one to the homeless.

REFLECT

A Check (✓) the Reflect activities you can do and the academic skills you can use.

- ☐ consider how a company can affect people's lives
- ☐ analyze data about social enterprise
- ☐ interpret statistics about disabilities
- ☐ present a social enterprise

- ☐ listen for definitions
- ☐ define and explain a concept
- ☐ quantifiers
- ☐ interpret statistics

B Write the vocabulary words from the unit in the correct column. Add any other words that you learned. Circle words you still need to practice.

NOUN	VERB	ADJECTIVE	ADVERB & OTHER

C Reflect on the ideas in the unit as you answer these questions.

1. What is a social enterprise and how can you support one?

_____

_____

2. What is the most important thing you learned in this unit?

_____

_____

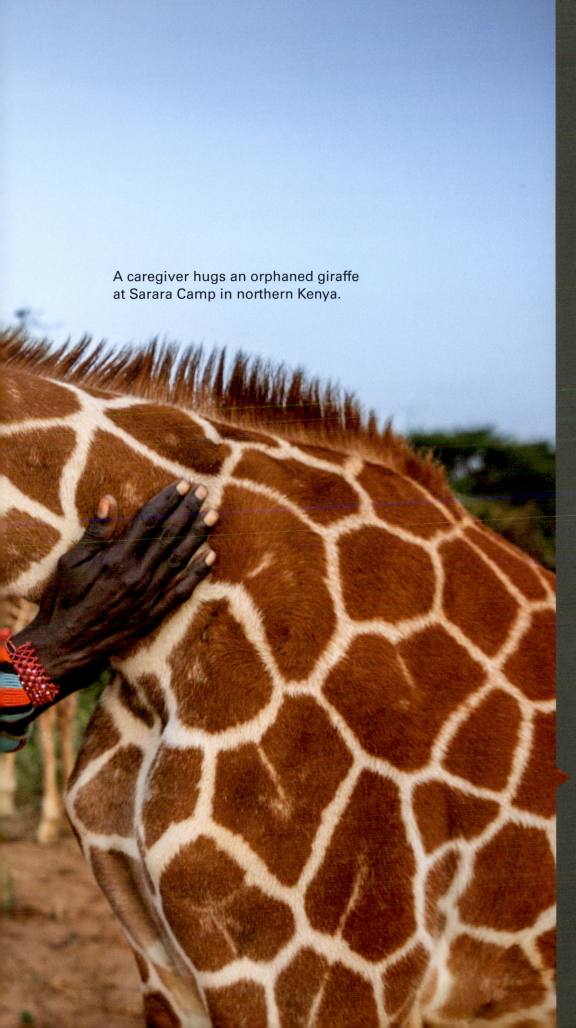

A caregiver hugs an orphaned giraffe at Sarara Camp in northern Kenya.

CONNECT TO THE TOPIC

1. How does the photo make you feel?
2. What do you think emotional intelligence is?

111

PREPARE TO LISTEN

A VOCABULARY Listen to the words. Work with a partner to match the two halves of each conversation. Then discuss what each word means. 🎧 7.1

1. _____ Do you wish you'd applied for that job?

2. _____ He doesn't believe he can do it.

3. _____ Do you think I was wrong to get angry?

4. _____ I'm sorry your son didn't get into medical school.

5. _____ Is it important to be aware of other people's feelings?

6. _____ I told her she couldn't come to the party.

7. _____ How did you do on the math test?

8. _____ Don't be so negative about your hopes of getting a job!

9. _____ Jessica was really annoyed about her vacation being canceled.

10. _____ Children always think everything is unfair when in fact it's just life.

a. I know. She **blames** the airline.

b. Yes, it was a big **disappointment** for him.

c. No, I don't. I'm not **judging** you in any way.

d. I **performed** much better than I expected.

e. Yes, but try to see it from their **perspective**.

f. Really? What was her **reaction**?

g. I'm not. I'm just trying to be **realistic**.

h. No, I don't have any **regrets**. I'm happy where I am.

i. I know. He isn't very **self-confident**.

j. Yes, I think it's a **weakness** not to notice other people's emotions.

B PERSONALIZE Discuss the questions with a partner. Explain your answers.

1. Would you say you are a positive, negative, or **realistic** person?

2. Do you often have **regrets** when you make a bad choice? Or do you forget it and move on?

3. When did you last **blame** someone for something that went wrong? Did you try to see things from their **perspective**?

4. If you **perform** badly at school or work, does it make you feel less **self-confident**?

5. Do you think showing your emotions can be a **weakness** sometimes?

C You will hear someone answering the last question in activity B. What is their view? 🎧 7.2

☐ It's a weakness.

☐ It's not a weakness.

☐ It depends.

Sometimes, when you answer a question, your ideas develop as you speak. Phrases like these are useful to show this thinking process:

That's an interesting question.　　　*But then again, . . .*
I think that depends.　　　　　　　*Perhaps it's not that simple.*
My first reaction is . . .　　　　　　*Maybe there's another way to look at it.*

D Read the Communication Tip. Then listen again and check (✓) the phrases you hear. 🎧 7.2

E Work with a new partner. Ask each other the first question in activity B. Think about what you said before and how you might express your idea more clearly this time. Use phrases from the Communication Tip.

REFLECT Describe your emotions.

You are going to listen to a lecture about emotional intelligence. Look at the photo. Imagine you are there. How does it make you feel? Are your emotions strong or not? Write the first word or words that come to mind. Then tell a partner what you wrote and why.

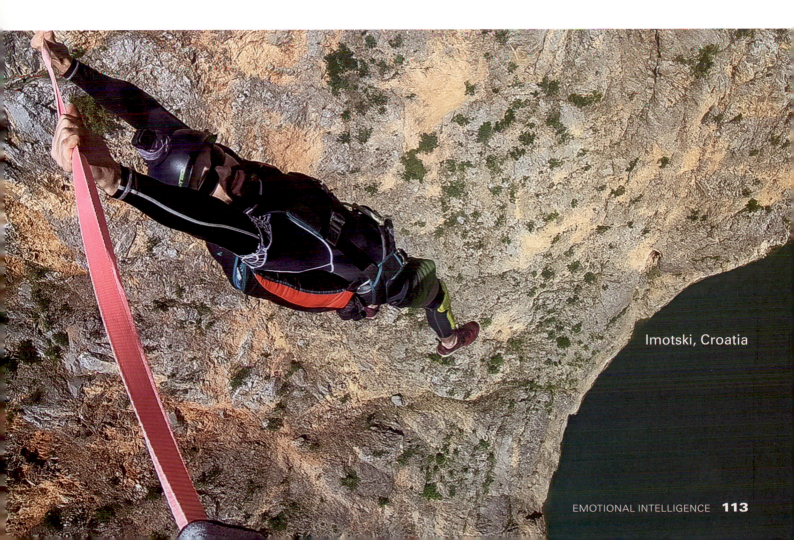

Imotski, Croatia

WHAT IS
EMOTIONAL
INTELLIGENCE?

Australia's rugby
team after a defeat
during the 2020
Olympics in Tokyo,
Japan

A PREVIEW Work with a partner to discuss the questions.

1. How do the men in the photo feel? Why?

2. Have you ever felt this way?

B MAIN IDEAS Read the questions. Then listen to the lecture and answer the questions. Compare your answers with a partner. 🎧 7.3

1. Who is Daniel Goleman?

   _____

2. What does he say emotional intelligence can help you do?

   _____

3. According to Goleman, these are the five elements that make up emotional intelligence. Number them in the order that you hear them.

   _____ a. self-regulation   _____ d. self-awareness

   _____ b. social skills   _____ e. empathy

   _____ c. internal motivation

C DETAILS Listen to part of the lecture. Complete the sentences. 🎧 7.4

1. If you ask a self-aware person to do something that they don't feel able to do, they will say _____.

2. If you're able to self-regulate, you'll move on quickly from a

   _____.

3. If you have internal motivation, you do things because you want to, not to earn _____.

4. If an empathetic person sees that someone looks unhappy after a work meeting, they'll ask, "Is _____?"

5. If you show that you appreciate other people, there's a better chance they'll want to _____ with you.

D Discuss the questions with a partner.

1. What did you know about emotional intelligence before listening to the lecture?

2. When do you think people start building their emotional intelligence?

3. Do you agree with Goleman that emotional intelligence will help you progress in your career?

4. Do you think emotional intelligence is as important as other kinds of intelligence?

E NOTICE THE GRAMMAR Think about the relationship between each pair of sentences. Then choose the correct word or phrase to connect them. With a partner, discuss what you think the words you chose mean.

1. People who are not self-aware sometimes agree to do things that they aren't good at and don't enjoy doing. **Consequently, / Instead,** they often fail and make themselves unhappy.

2. If you see someone is unhappy or worried, always ask them how they're feeling. **However, / Then** listen carefully to what they say, without judging them.

3. Having good social skills helps you to develop better relationships with people. **In contrast, / Obviously,** this is a very important quality in business where trust between people is essential.

4. People who can regulate their emotions often have a calm and positive attitude. **In contrast, / As a result,** people who cannot self-regulate have more up and down moods.

5. Don't just do activities that you have to do or that earn you money. **Then / Instead,** do things that motivate you personally and that you enjoy, too.

6. Emotional intelligence is an important part of our overall intelligence. **Consequently, / Indeed,** it is the most important factor in how successful we are.

7. Workers and leaders should understand what emotional intelligence is, **so / then** companies should offer training courses on it.

GRAMMAR Connectors

Connectors are words and phrases that help us connect ideas. Here are some connectors and the relationships they show:

▸ Comparing and contrasting: *However, On the other hand, In contrast, Instead*
▸ Emphasizing a point: *In fact, Indeed, Obviously, Moreover*
▸ Showing a sequence: *Then, Following that, Afterward, Next*
▸ Showing a result: *So, As a result, Consequently*

Sometimes these words come at the beginning of a sentence, and sometimes they join two parts of a sentence. Notice the punctuation.

*The smartest people are not always the most successful. **In fact,** research suggests that people with higher emotional intelligence have more satisfying lives.*

*In some situations, it's not appropriate to show your emotions. Always keeping emotions in, **however,** can hurt your health.*

F GRAMMAR Complete these sentences with your own ideas. Then compare with a partner.

1. Try not to judge people when they tell you their feelings. Instead, _____
   _____.

2. A leader should be good at understanding how people feel. Moreover, _____
   _____.

3. We can't stop ourselves from feeling certain emotions; however, _____
   _____.

4. Different cultures express their emotions in different ways. Consequently, _____
   _____.

5. There are times when you need to control your emotions. Obviously, _____
   _____.

6. Emotional intelligence helps us build more successful relationships. In fact, _____
   _____.

G Work with a small group. Listen to a conversation about how Liam reacted to a colleague's request for help. Answer the questions. Try to use connectors in your answers. 🎧 7.5

1. What can you say about Liam's emotional intelligence?
2. What can you say about Gary's emotional intelligence?
3. How could both colleagues deal with the situation differently in the future?
4. Have you ever been in a similar situation? What happened? How did you feel?

REFLECT Analyze your emotional intelligence.

Work with a small group. Use the emotions in the box and answer the questions. Give examples to illustrate your ideas.

anger	embarrassment	envy	nervousness	sadness

Which emotions do you find the easiest and the most difficult to:

a. notice in yourself?
b. manage when you feel them?
c. notice in other people?
d. react to and deal with when others express them?

PREPARE TO WATCH

A VOCABULARY Listen to the words. Complete the sentences with the words from the box that have the same meaning as the words in parentheses. Then discuss with a partner what each word means. 🎧 7.6

---

acknowledge (v)	confused (adj)	frustrated (adj)	handle (v)	overwhelmed (adj)
appropriately (adv)	expression (n)	genuinely (adv)	objective (adj)	work through (v phr)

---

1. Forget your personal feelings. Try to be _____ (fair).

2. I find angry people difficult to _____ (manage). I suppose it's because I'm easygoing myself.

3. I know you don't think it's a *big* problem. But can you just _____ (say you know) that it *is* a problem?

4. Why does she have that worried _____ (look) on her face?

5. I was _____ (really and truly) shocked when he said he was 25. He looks about 16!

6. We sometimes have difficulties in our relationship, but step by step we _____ (deal with) our problems.

7. Are you _____ (upset) that you haven't moved up quickly in your job at the bank?

8. Do you sometimes feel _____ (it's all too much) with everything that you have to do?

9. I never know how to respond _____ (in the right way) when people get angry.

10. I'm _____ (not clear in my mind) about my feelings. One part of me wants to go abroad to study; the other part is scared about it.

B Work with a partner. Act out short conversations, reading aloud five of the sentences in activity A and responding to them.

*A: Forget your personal feelings. Try to be **objective**.*

B: Yes, I know, but it's difficult because he's a good friend.

C PERSONALIZE Work with a partner. Answer the questions.

1. What makes you feel **frustrated**?

2. What do you do when you feel **overwhelmed**?

3. What can you do to **work through** a disagreement with someone?

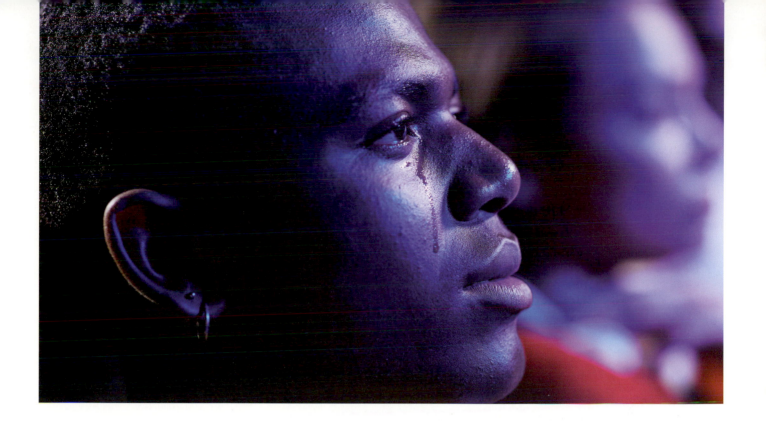

CRITICAL THINKING   Follow a line of reasoning

Critical thinking involves questioning things in a logical way. Following a logical line of reasoning will help you reach an answer. For example:

What is the person in the photo feeling? What could be causing him to feel this way? Why? Does my reasoning make sense based on previous experience?

D APPLY Work with a partner. Look at the photo and discuss how the person feels and what might be causing those feelings.

Consider ways of handling emotions.

You are going to watch a video on how to develop your emotional intelligence. Look at the infographic and answer the questions. Then discuss your answers with a partner.

How to Increase Your Emotional Intelligence

1. Be self-aware
How am I feeling right now? Am I comfortable with that?

2. Control your emotions
What would be a good reaction to this emotion?

3. Empathize
How is my partner feeling right now? How can I find out?

4. Practice social skills
How can I react to his/her feelings in a helpful way?

EMOTIONAL INTELLIGENCE:
NATURE OR NURTURE?

A teacher talks to a student
with stage fright before a play
in Johannesburg, South Africa.

A PREVIEW Look at the photo and read the caption. What might the teacher be saying? How can she use this moment to help build the student's emotional intelligence?

B PREDICT What do you think you can do to improve your emotional intelligence? Tell a partner. Then watch the video and check your predictions. ▶ 7.1

C MAIN IDEAS Choose the correct words to complete the sentences.

1. Start noticing your emotions and how they affect you **every morning / during the day**.

2. Manage your emotions and try to be **realistic / positive** about your feelings.

3. With negative thoughts, **allow them to come and go / analyze them**.

4. Show empathy by **listening quietly / listening and asking questions**.

5. Help others to **control / recognize** their own emotional reactions.

6. Learn to read people's **facial expressions / use of language**.

D PHRASES TO KNOW Work with a partner. Discuss the meaning of the phrases in bold from the video. Then answer the questions.

1. You felt stressed because you woke up late, and you knew you had **loads to do**.

   What's your first step when there is **loads to do**?

2. Sometimes it's difficult to **see a positive**. You're depressed because you didn't get that job you really wanted.

   Can you **see a positive** in not having a lot of money?

3. Showing empathy is a **key part of** emotional intelligence, too.

   What is a **key part of** being a good son or daughter?

E DETAILS Watch part of the video and complete the chart. ▶ 7.2

Feeling	Reason	Objective reaction
Stressed	Woke up late and had 1_____	You needed the 2_____.
3_____	Didn't know what your colleague was really 4_____	Most likely he was complimenting you.
5_____	Didn't get the 6_____ you wanted	Allow 7_____ thoughts to pass over you.
8_____	Boss never listens to 9_____	How would resigning make you feel?

F DETAILS Watch another part of the video and write the following. ▶ 7.3

1. The names of the four emotions that are mentioned: _____

_____

2. The name for small expressions that are difficult to notice: _____

3. The benefits of understanding these expressions: _____

_____

LISTENING SKILL Listen for connectors

As you learned, connectors are words and phrases that tell you how an idea relates to a previous one. Review the connectors and the relationships they show in the Grammar Box. Notice how the connectors help prepare you for what you will hear next.

Consequently introduces a result:

His internal motivation is high. **Consequently**, *he does not need to be pushed by his manager.*

In fact introduces an idea that emphasizes the previous one:

Showing empathy is a key part of emotional intelligence, too. **In fact,** *it's probably the most important aspect of how others see you.*

Instead introduces an alternative idea:

But you shouldn't be overwhelmed by negative thoughts. **Instead,** *just allow them to pass over you.*

G APPLY Work with a partner. Match the beginnings to the ends of the sentences. Then listen to check your answers. 🎧 7.7

1. _____ Don't just ignore your emotions. Instead,

2. _____ Your ability is an important factor in how successful you are; however,

3. _____ Recognizing expressions helps you understand others' feelings. Moreover,

4. _____ Becoming an active listener doesn't happen overnight. Obviously,

a. your attitude is probably more important.

b. it takes time.

c. try to notice how you're feeling.

d. it can help you notice your own feelings, too.

H Work with a small group. What positives can you find in these situations?

1. There is a lot of traffic on your way home from work or school.

2. Your boss/teacher gives you a short deadline to finish a project.

3. You get negative feedback on a project you did.

4. Your Internet isn't working. It's the weekend, and no one can fix it until Monday.

5. Your best friend moves to another country.

Use your emotional intelligence.

You are going to do some training on emotional intelligence. In the training, you will role-play a situation and listen as other students comment on it. You will then observe other students acting out a situation and comment on how they handle it. Use the ideas, vocabulary, and skills from the unit.

I MODEL Read the following situations. Then listen to people commenting on one of the situations. Which one are they are talking about? 🎧 7.8

1. Someone arrives at work to find that a new employee is sitting at their desk and has made themselves comfortable there. It's an open plan office (a large office space with no walls between people).

2. It's the end of the work day, and everyone is going out for pizza. One person wants to stay and finish her work. Another employee tries to make her come along.

3. At work, one employee, who is working hard, tells a colleague, who is having a break, to go and get him a coffee. The colleague is offended.

PRONUNCIATION Contrastive stress 🎧 7.9

In speech, it's common to use stress to emphasize a contrast. Heavy stress is placed on the word that highlights the contrast. For example:

1. A: He's upset that he wasn't picked for the team.
    B: But he **was** picked for the team.

2. A: Was she annoyed?
    B: No, she was **pleased**.

Note that the contrastive stress can be placed on structure words (as in 1 above) or on content words (as in 2 above).

J PRONUNCIATION Listen to the sentences from the conversation. Underline the word with contrastive stress in the second sentence in each pair. Then practice the conversations with a partner. 🎧 7.10

1. **Sara:** I gave him an angry look, but I didn't want to create a scene in the office.
    Anna: You didn't need to create a scene.

2. **Carl:** I don't know what you were thinking, Mark, speaking to her like that.
    Mark: Actually, I wasn't really thinking.

3. **Carl:** And you're both partly responsible for that.
    Mark: Actually, I think it's my responsibility to apologize first.

K PRONUNCIATION Underline the word showing contrastive stress in the second sentence in each pair. Then listen to check your answers. 🎧 7.11

1. **A:** Do you think he reacted badly?
   B: No, I think he was right to be angry.

2. **A:** I liked the way she handled the situation.
   B: Yes, but he didn't deal well with it at all.

3. **A:** He was quick to notice her feelings.
   B: Yes, but did he empathize with her?

4. **A:** The main problem with Jack is his temper.
   B: If you ask me, it's his attitude.

5. **A:** I blame myself for what happened.
   B: Don't. It's not your fault he got upset.

6. **A:** You're very good at recognizing your emotions.
   B: Now I just need to work on controlling them.

7. **A:** Are you nervous about the presentation?
   B: Actually, I'm excited about it.

L PRONUNCIATION Work with a partner. Write a response that has a word with contrastive stress. Then read the conversations aloud to the class.

1. **A:** Did you tell him the bad news?
   B: No, _____.

2. **A:** She often looks really bored.
   B: Yes, but _____.

3. **A:** The easiest emotion to recognize is happiness.
   B: Really? I think _____.

4. **A:** Talking about emotions is hard.
   B: _____.

SPEAKING SKILL   Make constructive comments

Often at school and at work, you will be asked to comment on things you've read and seen. It's important to express your comments in a constructive, or helpful, way. Here are some useful expressions for doing that:

I noticed/could see that you were angry.
Personally, I found/thought that you handled the situation well.
I wasn't sure why you treated her like that.
I liked the way that you encouraged him.
An area that you might work on is . . .
If it were me, I would/wouldn't (have) . . .

M APPLY Work with a partner. Think about the model in activity I. Discuss how Sara could have handled the situation differently after Mark told her to get him a coffee.

N APPLY Work with a partner. Comment on the following situations. Use phrases from the Speaking Skill box.

Situation	Comments
A colleague of yours, a science teacher, asks two students to do an experiment. He tells one that she should be in charge because she's so organized. He tells the other to watch and help if necessary. The second one looks disappointed.	
At work, Gianni asks his colleague Enrico to look at a letter he's written to a customer. Enrico thinks it's very badly written, but he tells him it's good because he doesn't want to offend Gianni.	
One of your classmates always arrives a few minutes late for class. When he enters the classroom, he greets the teacher, but the teacher is often annoyed and tells him to sit down and be quiet. Your classmate doesn't speak much for the rest of the class.	

Students in a science class at the Colégio Santo Agostinho Nova Lima in Belo Horizonte, Brazil

O PLAN Work with a partner. Use your emotional intelligence in a role-play about a possible conflict. Follow the steps below.

▶ Decide which situation to role-play.

Situation 1
Person 1 arrives at work to find that person 2, a new employee, is sitting at person 1's desk. It is an open plan office (a large office space with no walls between people).

Situation 2
It's the end of the work day, and everyone is going out for pizza. Person 1 wants to stay on and finish his/her work. Person 2 tries to make person 1 come along.

Situation 3
Person 1 tells a colleague about an idea he/she has for a new product. Later, at a team meeting, person 2, the colleague, says, "I have this great idea for a new product . . ."

▶ Decide what role you will each take and what you're going to say to each other.

▶ Decide what emotions you're going to express in words or through facial expressions.

Situation:	
What person 1 can say and do	**What person 2 can say and do**

P PRACTICE Practice acting out the situation with your partner. Give each other feedback to make your role-play stronger.

Q UNIT TASK Act out your situation for the class. Have the class guess what the situation is. Ask for constructive comments on how you handled the situation.

Observations	Comments
First, Jorge was surprised that Yuling sat at his desk, but he did not get angry.	*I liked the way that he controlled his feelings.*

REFLECT

A Check (✓) the Reflect activities you can do and the academic skills you can use.

☐ describe your emotions

☐ analyze your emotional intelligence

☐ consider ways of handling emotions

☐ use your emotional intelligence

☐ listen for connectors

☐ make constructive comments

☐ connectors

☐ follow a line of reasoning

B Write the vocabulary words from the unit in the correct column. Add any other words that you learned. Circle words you still need to practice.

NOUN	VERB	ADJECTIVE	ADVERB & OTHER

C Reflect on the ideas in the unit as you answer these questions.

1. What will you do to increase your emotional intelligence?

_____

_____

2. What is the most important thing you learned in this unit?

_____

_____

LEARNING FROM LIFE

International students learn to make tang yuan, or sweet dumplings, with a local homestay in Lin'an District, Hangzhou, Zhejiang Province, China.

CONNECT TO THE TOPIC

1. What else besides cooking do you think the students are learning?

2. What are some important lessons you have learned? Where did you learn them?

PREPARE TO LISTEN

A VOCABULARY Listen to the words in **bold**. Then read the sentences and discuss the meaning of these words with a partner. 🎧 8.1

1. Should university prepare you to become a subject specialist, **broaden** your general knowledge, or both?

2. Do you think it's better for a university to be on its own **campus** or in buildings spread around a city?

3. Do you have any tips for keeping your **concentration** when you're studying?

4. Are you **concerned** that competition for jobs will increase if more people go to university?

5. If you could **get involved in** any university sport or club, what would it be?

6. Which is more **intimidating**: speaking in front of teachers or speaking in front of friends and classmates?

7. How can a student **make the most of** their time at university?

8. Do you think **outgoing** people are more or less likely to be successful?

9. Which subjects or fields of study does a university need special **resources** for?

10. Which of these things would you **stress** to a new university student: getting good grades or enjoying the different opportunities available?

B Match the words from activity A with the correct definitions.

1. _____ broaden (v)	a. worried
2. _____ campus (n)	b. to give extra importance to
3. _____ concentration (n)	c. scary; threatening
4. _____ concerned (adj)	d. to become part of
5. _____ get involved in (v phr)	e. to use to the best advantage
6. _____ intimidating (adj)	f. sociable; not shy
7. _____ make the most of (v phr)	g. attention
8. _____ outgoing (adj)	h. a special area for school buildings
9. _____ resource (n)	i. to widen
10. _____ stress (v)	j. something needed to do a job or task

C PERSONALIZE Work with a partner to ask and answer five of the questions in activity A. Give reasons for your answers.

D Work with a small group. Imagine you are about to study abroad at a university. Discuss what things you would feel excited or nervous about.

E Listen to someone speak about her move to a foreign university. Is she excited and nervous about the same things as you? 🎧 8.2

Moving in day for new students at Macalester College in Saint Paul, Minnesota, USA

CRITICAL THINKING   Be aware of the whole picture

When you hear or read information, you, of course, need to evaluate the information given, but you should also think about what information is *not* given. By including only some of the facts, the writer or speaker can give a biased or uneven view.

For example, an infographic showing the rising cost of going to a university does not show that other costs of living are increasing at the same rate. It is only giving part of the picture.

REFLECT   Discuss challenges for students entering a new school.

Before you listen to someone give advice to new college students, imagine you are about to enter a new school. Work with a small group. Look at the chart and answer the questions. Then share your ideas with the class.

Issues Faced by Students at a New School

Practical	Emotional	Cultural & Social
Getting around Finding a place to live Managing expenses	Having self-confidence Letting go of expectations Feeling stress about homework	Making friends Getting used to different teaching styles Balancing schoolwork and fun

1. Are any of these possible issues relevant to you? Explain.

2. What other issues do you think international students might face? Add them to the appropriate columns.

3. Do you think the chart presents the whole picture or does it give only part of the picture? Explain.

LISTEN & SPEAK
ADVICE TO MY FIRST-YEAR SELF

University students in Dubai, United Arab Emirates

A PREDICT You will hear a former student give a welcome talk to new international students at a college. Check (✓) what you think he will do in his talk. Then check your predictions after you listen.

☐ Give practical advice   ☐ Suggest they try new things
☐ Give them study tips   ☐ Talk about the local culture
☐ Make them feel welcome   ☐ Warn them about certain teachers

B MAIN IDEAS Listen to the talk. Work with a partner to summarize the talk in one or two sentences. 🎧 8.3

_____

_____

C DETAILS Read the statements. Listen to the talk again. Write T for *True*, F for *False*, or NG for *Not Given*. 🎧 8.3

According to Hassan, . . .

1. _____ if you don't get enough sleep, you'll feel stressed and unable to concentrate.
2. _____ if you get involved in activities, you'll get to meet different people.
3. _____ if you find out about people, you'll become interested in them and make friends.
4. _____ if you ask people questions, they'll ignore you.
5. _____ if you don't understand a lecture, you can listen to it again online.
6. _____ if you fill your time with different activities, you'll find the work easier, too.

D Imagine you are a new student at the welcome talk. You are given this evaluation form. Complete it and then compare your answers with a partner.

	Very	Somewhat	Not at all
The talk was clear.			
The talk was interesting.			
The advice was useful.			
The talk covered the points I needed it to.			
How could the talk have been improved?			

E Present your conclusions to the class. What other things would you have liked to hear about?

GRAMMAR Noun clauses

A noun clause acts as a noun. We can use a noun clause instead of a noun or noun phrase.

           noun phr   noun phr
I stressed <u>the risks</u>. / I don't understand <u>your question</u>.

                noun clause   noun clause
*I stressed **that it was risky**. / I don't understand **what you're asking**.*

We form noun clauses with *that* or a *wh-* word (*who, what, which, where, when, why,* or *how*) + subject + verb:

> *I expect **that she'll complete the course**.*
> *I know **where she lives**.*
> *She explained **why we had to listen to the lecture twice**.*

Note that noun clauses with *wh-* words use statement word order, *not* question word order.

What or *which* in noun clauses can be followed immediately by a noun or noun phrase:

> *I don't remember **what kind of shoes he was wearing**.*

How in noun clauses can be followed immediately by an adjective or adverb:

> *I'd like to know **how old the building is**.*
> *I was amazed at **how quickly he learned**.*

F GRAMMAR Unscramble the words in *italics* to complete these sentences from the talk.

1. I remember *felt I how.*

   _____

2. I can't stress enough *how this is important.*

   _____

3. I know *can it that be intimidating.*

   _____

4. I thought *accent my people that understand wouldn't.*

   _____

5. Maybe you're worried that you won't understand *your professor is saying what.*

   _____

6. My message is not *that unimportant is the work.*

   _____

7. You will miss a very important part of *what life is about student.*

   _____

8. Every experience feeds into *you will who become.*

   _____

9. Don't forget *more than are just your schoolwork you that.*

   _____

G GRAMMAR Rewrite each underlined noun phrase as a noun clause with the same meaning. Use the correct form of the words in parentheses.

1. I agree with <u>his point of view</u>.

   I agree with (what / say) _what he says_.

2. She prefers <u>her old college</u>.

   She prefers (where / study) _____.

3. I am hoping for <u>good grades</u>.

   I am hoping (that / get) _____.

4. It depends on <u>your pronunciation of the word</u>.

   It depends on (how / pronounce) _____.

5. People don't appreciate <u>his intelligence</u>.

   People don't appreciate (how / be) _____.

6. We understand <u>your concerns</u>.

   We understand (that / be) _____.

7. Have you decided on <u>a university</u> yet?

   Have you decided (which / go to) _____?

8. I couldn't understand <u>his reaction</u>.

   I couldn't understand (why / react) _____.

REFLECT   Reflect on important transitions in life.

Look at the word cloud showing important transition points in life. Discuss the questions with a partner. Try to use noun clauses in your answers.

Going to college   **Having a child**   **Starting elementary school**   Moving to a new home   **Changing jobs**   **Leaving home**   **Becoming an adult**   Getting your first job   **Getting married**

1. Which transitions have you already experienced? How did you feel about them at the time? How did these transitions change you?

2. Which transitions are you excited about? Which are you nervous about? Give reasons.

PREPARE TO WATCH

A VOCABULARY Listen to the words in **bold**. Match the questions and statements with the responses. Then discuss with a partner what each word in **bold** means. 🎧 8.4

1. _____ Are you thinking of studying **academic** subjects at college?
2. _____ I recommend the National University of Singapore. But that's my own personal **bias**.
3. _____ Why is developing **discipline** important for students?
4. _____ Are you waiting to see what job opportunities **emerge** after you graduate?
5. _____ Do you think a **formal** education is important for everyone?
6. _____ Your sister gets amazing results at college. Is she very **hard-working**?
7. _____ Our school always put a lot of focus on the **individual**.
8. _____ When did your brother **quit** school?
9. _____ What's the **state** of the classrooms?
10. _____ When you study history, how do you find the **truth** about what happened?

a. Not really. She doesn't study more than other people. She's just very clever.

b. Yes. I don't have a particular job in mind.

c. As soon as he could. At 16 he went to work as a mechanic in a garage.

d. Why? Were you a student there yourself?

e. Really? I think it's better to put the needs of the group first.

f. No. I'm going to a technical college instead to become a chef.

g. They need to be able to stay focused on their work even when there are distractions.

h. It depends on the person. For some, real-world experiences might be more useful.

i. It's difficult. But you have to listen to all sides of the story.

j. Terrible. They haven't been painted for 10 years.

B PERSONALIZE Discuss the questions with a partner.

1. What is the earliest age that a student can **quit** formal education in your country?

2. How **hard-working** are/were you at school? Do/Did you have to work harder at some **academic** subjects than others?

3. Do/Did your parents have any **biases** about what you should study?

4. Do you have any advice for people who can't find the **discipline** to study by themselves?

When you explain why something is important, it's helpful to describe the benefits that it brings. To do this, use words and phrases such as:

It provides a useful qualification.

It can (really) help (to) give you access to a lot of jobs.

Without it, you can't get into college.

It enables you to study a wide range of subjects.

C Listen to someone talking about why education is important. Which reason in the infographic below does the speaker discuss? 🎧 8.5

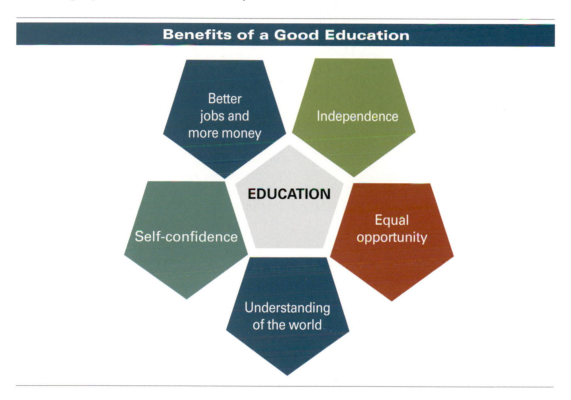

Benefits of a Good Education

- Better jobs and more money
- Independence
- EDUCATION
- Equal opportunity
- Understanding of the world
- Self-confidence

D Work with a partner. Discuss which benefits in the infographic above are most relevant to you. Use the phrases in the Communication Tip to help you. Then work with another pair and compare your answers.

REFLECT   Compare the value of education and experience.

You are going to watch a video about a successful artist and National Geographic Explorer who decided against going to college. Discuss the questions in a small group.

1. How does having a formal education benefit a person looking for a job?

2. How does having real-world experience benefit people looking for a job?

3. Which do you think will help you more in the long run: formal education or real-world experience? Explain.

NEW WAYS OF LOOKING AND LEARNING

National Geographic
Explorer Raghava KK

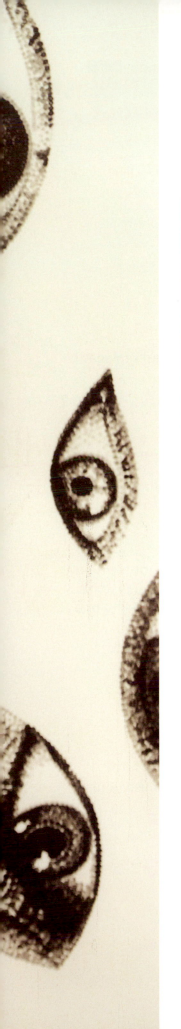

A PREVIEW Artist and National Geographic Explorer Raghava KK makes art that his viewers can participate in. Watch an excerpt from the video and answer the questions. ▶ 8.1

1. What happens to Mona Lisa 2.0? Why?
2. How does this technology change the experience of viewing art?

LISTENING SKILL Identify key phrases and sentences

The important ideas in a talk are often summed up in key phrases or sentences. To identify these key phrases and sentences, listen for these features:

- They are often short and memorable.
- The words or ideas in them are repeated or rephrased.
- The speaker may pause before saying them.
- The speaker may say them more slowly.

For example: *Education is what a system does to you; learning is what you do to yourself. Education is supposed to lead to learning.*

From these two sentences, you know that two important ideas of the talk are *education* and *learning.*

B APPLY Read the key phrases and sentences in bold. Then watch the whole video and number them in the order you hear them (1–4). ▶ 8.2

a. _____ . . . I quit formal education after high school **to pursue learning where the world was my classroom** . . . I've always seen myself as an explorer.

b. _____ I want to see the emergence of a third form of knowledge. One in which multiple truths coexist . . . **truth for me is about perspectives.**

c. _____ I want to show you my latest art project that **brings live perspectives to my art** . . . you're going to participate to bring my work to life.

d. _____ **There's a big difference between learning and education.** Education is what a system does to you; learning is what you do to yourself.

C MAIN IDEAS Choose the three statements that express Raghava's main points.

a. He comes from a scientific background.
b. Education and learning are not the same thing.
c. If you want a real education, quit school.
d. To learn the truth, you have to look at things from different perspectives.
e. He wants viewers to participate with his art to make it come alive.

D DETAILS Watch the video again and choose two correct answers for each question. ▶8.2

1. How does Raghava describe his family?

   a. academic   b. interesting   c. scientific

2. What is real education about, according to his father?

   a. learning how to learn   b. being curious   c. fighting against discipline

3. Which of these things did the young Raghava decide?

   a. to go to art college   b. to quit school   c. to be financially independent

4. What are the different roles that Raghava has?

   a. a businessman   b. a computer programmer   c. a politician

5. What mental states was Raghava trying to get the photo to reflect?

   a. calm   b. happiness   c. interest

E PHRASES TO KNOW Work with a partner. Choose which word or phrase can replace the bold phrase from the video in each sentence. Then answer the questions.

1. Do you think education **is supposed to** lead to a good job?

   a. should   b. could

2. Do you **have an issue with** any parts of formal education?

   a. have an interest in   b. have a problem with

3. What kind of person do you **see yourself as**?

   a. think you are   b. want to be

F Raghava KK is a successful artist and businessman who did not go to college. But not everyone who quits formal education is as successful as he is. Work with a small group to discuss what other factors in Raghava's life could have contributed to his success. Use the categories below and any other ideas you have.

▸ Family

▸ Friends

▸ Personality

▸ Other: _____

G Raghava says he plays different roles in his life. What are the different roles that *you* have in your life? What have you learned from these roles? Complete the chart. Then discuss your answers in a small group.

Role	What I have learned
▸ Brother	▸ How important family is
▸	▸
▸	▸

Share a memorable learning experience.

A local arts and education center is putting on an exhibition called "Education in the Community." One exhibit will be a video of students sharing their most memorable learning experiences. You are going to take part. Use the ideas, vocabulary, and skills from the unit.

H MODEL Listen to someone talking about her most memorable learning experience. Then answer the questions. 🎧 8.6

1. What does the speaker say generally makes a memorable learning experience?

   _____

2. What did the teacher ask the students to do?

   _____

3. What did the speaker write about?

   _____

4. How did she feel about the experience afterward?

   _____

I Work with a small group to discuss the questions.

1. What are the benefits of doing something outside of your comfort zone?
2. What are the benefits of feeling comfortable and safe when learning?

Young people take cooking lessons from a chef in São Paulo, Brazil.

PRONUNCIATION   Thought groups and pausing 🎧 8.7

When we explain or describe something, we naturally pause between certain chunks of language. A "chunk" could be:

▸ A short statement: *I have no idea.*; *I loved that teacher.*
▸ A clause: *when we arrived*; *if you think about it*; *who used to teach us every day*
▸ A noun or prepositional phrase: *the big green house*; *in the first place*

In the following example, the pauses are marked with a slash (/):

   She's the most creative teacher / that I've ever had / by far.

J   PRONUNCIATION Listen to this sentence from the model. The speaker pauses two times. Mark the pauses with a slash (/). Then compare your answers with a partner. 🎧 8.8

She asked us all to write and perform a short poem or a rap about something we

really cared about.

K   PRONUNCIATION Look at this part of the model. Practice saying it, thinking about where the pauses could go. (There is no right or wrong answer to this.) Then listen and compare your ideas to the version you hear. 🎧 8.9

And I didn't know what to write about. But then I thought, "I'll write about all

the people who have made a difference in my life." And when I read my poem,

everyone in the class clapped and I felt amazing.

L   PRONUNCIATION Answer the questions. Mark where you think pauses should go. Then work with a partner. Have your partner read your sentences with the pauses you marked. Do they sound good to you? Make adjustments to the pauses as needed.

1. Who is your favorite teacher, and why?

   _____

2. How do you learn best?

   _____

3. What was a challenging assignment you did?

   _____

4. What have you taught someone, and why?

   _____

When you listen to a description or explanation, you may need to check that you've understood the information properly. You can do this by highlighting the point and then asking for clarification. You should never be afraid to ask for clarification. Use phrases and questions such as:

I didn't quite get what you said about . . .
I didn't follow the part about . . .
I'm not sure I understood an expression you used.
When you said . . ., what (exactly) did you mean by that?
Could you explain/say a bit more about . . .?
Could you give an example?

M APPLY Listen again to the last part of the model. One of the people in the audience asks a question about something he didn't understand. Complete the question and answer. 🎧8.10

B: Thank you for sharing that. It sounds amazing. There was just one thing I

¹_____. You said that you learn when you do things

that are outside of your comfort zone. What

²_____ ?

A: Well, ³_____ certain tasks or assignments feel really

easy to complete? That's because they're in your comfort zone. They feel

familiar and safe. Things that are outside of your comfort zone can make you

feel a little uncomfortable. ⁴_____ I grow a lot when

I need to take a risk and do something new or different.

N APPLY Work with a partner. Look at the statements below. Take turns asking and answering questions about the words and phrases in bold to check understanding. Use a dictionary to look up any words you don't know.

> My favorite teacher was a **substitute teacher** we had for one semester.

> We had to do a project that involved interviewing **health care workers**.

> I made a model of an airplane out of **Plasticine**, and I was so proud of it.

> I was bad at drawing, so the teacher said I could **make a collage** instead.

O PLAN Take notes in the chart below about your most memorable learning experience. Think carefully about what you are going to say.

Where and when did it happen?	
What did you have to do?	
How did you feel beforehand?	
What made it a special experience?	
What did you learn?	
How did you feel afterward?	

P PRACTICE Describe your learning experience to a partner. Use pauses to make your description sound clear and natural. Ask your partner for feedback to help you with the final presentation.

Q UNIT TASK Share your most memorable learning experience with the class. Answer any questions. Be sure to ask your classmates questions about anything you don't understand in their presentations. Then vote on which experiences should be sent to the exhibition. Use the criteria below or create your own.

- ▶ Most unusual
- ▶ Most fun
- ▶ Biggest lesson learned
- ▶ Best outcome

REFLECT

A Check (✓) the Reflect activities you can do and the academic skills you can use.

☐ discuss challenges for students entering a new school

☐ reflect on important transitions in life

☐ compare the value of education and experience

☐ share a memorable learning experience

☐ identify key phrases and sentences

☐ ask for clarification

☐ noun clauses

☐ be aware of the whole picture

B Write the vocabulary words from the unit in the correct column. Add any other words that you learned. Circle words you still need to practice.

NOUN	VERB	ADJECTIVE	ADVERB & OTHER

C Reflect on the ideas in the unit as you answer these questions.

1. What are some important ideas to remember about learning and education?

_____

_____

2. What is the most important thing you learned in this unit?

_____

_____

Suffixes *-al, -ial,* and *-ical*

Suffixes come at the end of words. You can add the suffixes *-al, -ial,* and *-ical* to some nouns to form adjectives. If the noun ends in *-y* or *-e,* drop the last letter before adding the suffix. If the noun ends in *-ce,* you may need to change the *-ce* to *-t* and add *-ial.* Check a dictionary for the correct spelling.

> industry + **ial** = **industrial**
> history + **ical** = **historical**
> essence + **ial** = **essential**

A Write the correct adjective form of the nouns. Check your answers in a dictionary.

1. type _____
2. person _____
3. culture _____
4. environment _____
5. education _____
6. emotion _____

7. part _____
8. season _____
9. substance _____
10. option _____
11. psychology _____
12. transformation _____

B Complete each sentence with an adjective from activity A.

1. Leaving home to go to college made me very _____. I was both happy and sad.

2. Beach towns often experience _____ changes in population, with many more people during the summer.

3. I have a _____ connection to Japan. My mother was born there.

4. The museum offers _____ programs, such as earth sciences courses.

5. If you need to cancel your reservation, you can get a _____ refund, but it's too late to get all of the money back.

6. On a _____ weekend, I usually sleep late and then do something with my friends.

7. Many people say that the college experience is _____; it really changes you.

8. The advanced course is _____. You don't have to take it, but it's a good opportunity to learn more about the topic.

9. Most people are aware of the _____ dangers of plastic waste.

Prefixes *il-, im-, in-, ir-,* and *un-*

Prefixes come at the beginning of words. You can add a prefix to a word to change its meaning. You can add the prefixes *il-, im-, in-, ir-,* and *un-* to some adjectives to give them the opposite meaning. Use *ir-* before adjectives beginning with *r, il-* before adjectives beginning with *l,* and *im-* before adjectives beginning with *p* or *m.*

> **ir** + *regular* = **irregular**, meaning "not regular"
> **in** + *convenient* = **inconvenient**, meaning "not convenient"
> **il** + *legal* = **illegal**, meaning "not legal"
> **im** + *possible* = **impossible**, meaning "not possible"
> **un** + *believable* = **unbelievable**, meaning "not believable"

Note that there are exceptions to these rules. Check a dictionary for the correct spelling.

A Write the correct prefix to make the opposite meaning of the words.

1. _____ complicated

2. _____ logical

3. _____ original

4. _____ predictable

5. _____ replaceable

6. _____ significant

7. _____ suitable

8. _____ patient

B Complete each sentence with a word from activity A.

1. That argument doesn't make sense. It's _____.

2. The ideas in that song are not new. They are _____.

3. Great works of art are unique. If they get damaged, they are _____.

4. Jeans and t-shirts are usually _____ clothing for job interviews.

5. I need directions that are _____. If they are too difficult, I will get lost.

6. In this area, weather in the spring is _____. It might snow, or it might be sunny and warm.

7. The difference between the two salaries was _____, so I took the job I liked more.

8. Don't be _____. Just wait for your turn.

Phrasal verbs With *come*

A phrasal verb is a two- or three-word verb phrase. It always contains one verb and at least one other small word called a "particle." Phrasal verbs sometimes have multiple meanings. Some are easy to guess—for example, *come up* can mean "to come towards, approach." Some meanings can be less obvious—for example, *come up* can also mean "to happen" or "to become known suddenly." Use context to help you understand the correct meaning.

A Read the sentences. Use the context to choose the correct meaning.

1. How is your English **coming along**? What can help you to improve quickly?

   a. to go with someone   b. to make progress   c. to happen or show up

2. How easy is it for you to **come around** to ideas that are different than yours?

   a. to agree with   b. to happen again   c. to visit

3. Does your family **come before** work and school?

   a. to happen first   b. to appear in front of   c. to be more important than

4. Has an argument ever **come between** you and a good friend? What happened?

   a. to cause disagreement   b. to be lost   c. to prevent you from doing something

5. I think good communication **comes down to** using clear language. Do you agree?

   a. to depend on   b. to go down   c. to become yours

6. What feelings **come over** you at special times of the year?

   a. to visit   b. to affect   c. to move from a place

7. Have you **come through** any difficult situations in your life? What helped you?

   a. to arrive   b. to do what is expected   c. to survive

B Ask and answer the questions in activity A with a partner.

C Choose three phrasal verbs from activity A and write one sentence for each.

Suffix -ize

The suffix -ize means "to make or become." It can be added to some nouns and adjectives to form verbs.

N V
revolution + **ize** = revolution**ize**

ADJ V
special + **ize** = special**ize**

A Complete the chart with the correct missing forms. Use a dictionary to help you.

Noun	Verb	Adjective
		conceptual
individual		
		maximum
		personal
		real
		social
symbol		

B Complete the sentences with the correct form of the verbs from the chart.

1. I want to _____ my dorm room so it doesn't look like all the others.

2. Lena is rather shy. She doesn't like to _____ with a lot of people.

3. I love this picture from my time at college. It really _____ the experience.

4. It's hard for me to _____ an idea without having a model to look at.

5. With more than fifty percent of the votes counted, everyone _____ who the winner was.

6. I want to _____ the time I have in Kyoto and see as many sights as I can.

Polysemy

Polysemy refers to a word or phrase that has two or more different meanings. Sometimes the meanings are similar but not exactly the same. They are often different parts of speech.

*There is a lot of plastic **waste** in the oceans.* (n)
*I just **wasted** an hour trying to fix my computer.* (v)

Use context clues—the words around the word—to help you choose the correct meaning.

A Choose the best meaning for the words in bold. Use context clues to help.

estimate a. (v) to give a rough measure of value, cost, size, etc.; b. (n) a rough guess; c. (n) a statement of the cost of something; d. (n) an opinion of someone or something

1. _____ I received an **estimate**. The repair will cost about $200.

2. _____ Scientists try to measure the amount of plastic in the ocean, but sometimes they have to **estimate.**

3. _____ My **estimate** of Hana's work has changed. I think she's doing a great job.

make up a. (v) to form something; b. (v) to invent something, often not true; c. (v) to put something on someone's face to change their looks

4. _____ When I was little, I **made up** stories about people on other planets.

5. _____ The people who **make up** actors on movies sometimes win awards.

6. _____ Plastic bags **make up** at least 10% of the plastic in oceans.

stuff a. (n) a general term for things; b. (v) to fill with something; c. (v) to fill (oneself) with a lot of food

7. _____ It's so hard to move to a different city. We have so much **stuff.**

8. _____ After a long soccer practice, Jack and Miko sometimes **stuff** themselves.

9. _____ I **stuffed** my backpack with everything I needed for school—books, notebooks, my lunch, and a jacket.

run a. (v) to move at a faster speed than walking; b. (v) to operate; c. (n) an act of running; d. (n) a continuous period or series of things

10. _____ The machine is not running properly. We need to get it fixed.

11. _____ We had a run of bad luck on our trip. We missed our first flight, our hotel was noisy, and the weather was bad.

12. _____ How long have you been running in races?

Prefixes *em-, en-,* and *trans-*

The prefixes *em-* and *en-* mean "to cause to be" or "to put into or onto."

> *em* + *power* = **empower**, meaning "to cause someone to be stronger"
> *en* + *able* = **enable**, meaning "to cause to be able"
> *en* + *danger* = **endanger**, meaning "to put into danger"

The prefix *trans-* means "to change" or "to carry across."

> *trans* + *form* = **transform**, meaning "to change form"
> *trans* + *act* = **transact**, meaning "to do business with another person or company"

A Work with a partner to write a definition for each word. Check your answers in a dictionary.

1. employ (v) _____

2. enrage (v) _____

3. enrich (v) _____

4. translate (v) _____

5. transport (v) _____

B Complete each sentence with the correct form of a word from the box.

embolden	enable	envision	transfer	transform	transition

1. Wearing different types of glasses can _____ the way you look.

2. Make sure you _____ your microphone before the video conference.

3. The drawing of the house helps people _____ what it will look like.

4. I need to _____ to a different class. This one is too hard.

5. The success of the business _____ the owner to open another store.

6. Many people enjoy their commute as a nice _____ between home and work.

Collocations *Acknowledge, handle,* and *perform* + noun

Collocations are two or more words that often go together. It is useful to learn collocations in the same way you learn an individual word. The verbs *acknowledge, handle,* and *perform* collocate with particular nouns.

acknowledge	handle	perform
the difficulty	a call	a ceremony (like a wedding)
a fact	a complaint	a duty
guilt	an inquiry	an experiment
the importance	a request	an operation/surgery
a mistake	a situation	a role
one's responsibility	stress	a dance

A Complete the conversations using the correct form of the collocations from the box above. More than one answer may be possible.

1. A: Someone called to complain about the noise in Apartment 3G.

   B: How did you _____?

2. A: My cousin is getting married, and she asked me to _____.

   B: Wow, that's a big responsibility!

3. A: How did the scientists discover the medicine worked?

   B: They _____.

4. A: What did the store manager do when you complained that you received the wrong product?

   B: He _____ and gave me my money back.

5. A: My roommates got into a big argument over the weekend, and I didn't want to be part of it.

   B: How did you _____?

6. A: As employees, we are feeling overwhelmed with all of the changes in the company. What are you going to do to help us?

   B: We _____ and will provide more training and better communication immediately.

B Write a sentence using a collocation with each verb in your notebook.

Phrases With *get* and *make*

The verbs *get* and *make* are part of many phrases and idioms. Learn the meaning of the phrase as a whole unit.

get	make
a feeling/idea/impression	the best/most of
on someone's nerves	a difference
involved in	ends meet
a grip	matters worse
your (own) way	sense

A Underline the phrases with *get* and *make* in the sentences. Then match each phrase to its definition.

1. _____ Did you get the impression that Jung was upset?

2. _____ Can you stop bouncing that ball? It's getting on my nerves.

3. _____ Ben always wants to get his own way. He doesn't even try to agree with others.

4. _____ You've really got to get a grip. Don't get so upset about little things.

5. _____ Wow! That new paint really makes a difference in here.

6. _____ Please don't say anything to the teacher. It will only make matters worse.

7. _____ Elena's reaction doesn't make sense to me. Can you explain it?

8. _____ My job doesn't pay much. I sometimes have trouble making ends meet.

a. to try to control your emotions and act more calmly

b. to form an opinion about something based on what you notice

c. to improve a situation

d. to have enough money to pay for what you need

e. to annoy someone, especially by doing something over and over again

f. to make a situation more difficult

g. to have a meaning you can understand

h. to do what you want even if others disagree

B Answer the questions with a partner.

1. What gets on your nerves?

2. In what situations can getting upset make matters worse?

3. What can you do to make a difference in your community?

VOCABULARY INDEX

*Academic words

VOCABULARY INDEX

NOTE-TAKING SKILLS

Taking clear notes will improve your understanding and retention of the ideas you hear. Because you need to interpret your own notes, it's important to develop a system that works for you. However, there are some common strategies to improve your note taking.

BEFORE YOU LISTEN

▸ Focus: Try to clear your mind before the speaker begins so you can pay attention. If possible, review previous notes or think about what you already know about the topic.

▸ Predict: If you know the topic of the talk, think about what you might hear.

WHILE YOU LISTEN

▸ Take notes by hand: Research suggests that taking notes by hand rather than on a computer is more effective. Taking notes by hand requires you to summarize, rephrase, and synthesize information. This helps you encode the information (put it into a form that you can understand and remember).

▸ Listen for organizational clues: Speakers often use organizational clues (e.g., *We'll start by . . ., then . . ., and finally . . .*) to organize their ideas and show relationships between them. Listening for organizational clues can help you decide what information to write in your notes. For example, if you hear "There are three important factors to consider," you can write 1–3 so that you are ready to take note of the three factors.

▸ Condense (shorten) information:

  • As you listen, focus on the most important ideas. The speaker will usually repeat, define, explain, and/or give examples of these ideas. Take notes on these ideas.

  • Don't write full sentences. Write only key words (nouns, verbs, adjectives, and adverbs), phrases, or short sentences.

  • Leave out information that is obvious.

  • Write numbers and statistics using numerals (e.g., *9 bil; 35%*).

  • Use abbreviations (e.g., *ft., min., yr.*) and symbols (=, ≠, >, <, %, →).

  • Use indenting to show different levels of importance. Write main ideas on the left side of the paper. Indent details.

  • Write details under key terms to help you remember them.

  • Write the definitions of important new words.

AFTER YOU LISTEN

▸ Review your notes soon after the lecture or presentation. Add any details you missed.

▸ Clarify anything you don't understand in your notes with a classmate or teacher.

▸ Add or highlight main ideas. Cross out details that aren't important or necessary.

▸ Rewrite anything that is hard to read or understand. Rewrite your notes in an outline or other graphic organizer to organize the information more clearly.

▸ Use arrows, boxes, diagrams, or other visual cues to show relationships between ideas.

ORGANIZING INFORMATION

You can use a graphic organizer to take notes while you are listening, or to organize your notes after you listen. Here are some examples of graphic organizers.

FLOWCHARTS are used to show processes, or cause/effect relationships.

OUTLINES show the relationship between main ideas and details. You can make an outline as you listen or go back and rewrite your notes as an outline later.

First main point: _____

    Supporting info: _____

Second main point: _____

    Supporting info: _____

Third main point: _____

    Supporting info: _____

Conclusion: _____

MIND MAPS show the connection between concepts. The main idea is usually in the center with supporting ideas and details around it.

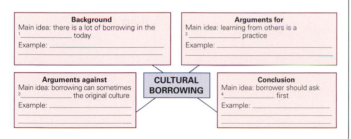

VENN DIAGRAMS compare and contrast two or more topics. The overlapping areas show similarities.

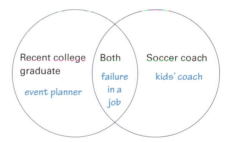

TIMELINES show a sequence of events.

T-CHARTS compare two topics.

Pros	Cons

USEFUL PHRASES

Clarifying/checking your understanding

So are you saying that. . .?
So what you mean is. . .?
What do you mean?
How so?
I'm not sure I understand/follow.
Do you mean. . .?
I'm not sure what you mean.

Asking for clarification/confirming understanding

I'm not sure I understand the question.
I'm not sure I understand what you mean.
Sorry, I'm not following you.
Are you saying that. . .?
If I understand correctly, you're saying that. . .

Checking others' understanding

Does that make sense?
Do you understand?
Do you see what I mean?
Is that clear?
Are you following/with me?
Do you have any questions?

Asking for opinions

What do you think?
Do you have anything to add?
What are your thoughts?
How do you feel?
What's your opinion?

Taking turns

Can/May I say something?
Could I add something?
Can I just say. . .?
May I continue?
Can I finish what I was saying?
Did you finish your thought?
Let me finish.

Interrupting politely

Excuse me.
Pardon me.
Forgive me for interrupting. . .
I hate to interrupt, but. . .
Can I stop you for a second?

Asking for repetition

Could you say that again?
I'm sorry?
I didn't catch what you said.
I'm sorry. I missed that. What did you say?
Could you repeat that, please?

Showing interest

I see. Good for you.
Really? Seriously?
Um-hmm. No kidding!
Wow. And? (Then what?)
That's funny/amazing/incredible/awful!

Giving reasons or causes

Because/Since + (clause)
Because of/Due to + (noun phrase)
The reason is (that) + (clause)
One reason is (that) + (clause)
The main reason is (that) + (clause)

Giving results or effects

. . ., so + (clause)
Therefore,/As a result,/Consequently, + (sentence)
. . . causes/leads to + (noun phrase)
. . . had an impact/effect on + (noun phrase)
If + (clause), then + (clause),

Identifying a side track

On a different subject, . . .
As an aside, . . .
That reminds me, . . .
This is off-topic, but . . .

Returning to a previous topic

Getting back to our previous discussion, . . .
To return to our earlier topic, . . .
So, to return to what we were saying, . . .
OK, getting back on topic, . . .

INDEX OF EXAM SKILLS & TASKS

Reflect is designed to provide practice for standardized exams, such as IELTS and TOEFL. This book has many activities that focus on and practice skills and question types that are needed for test success.

CREDITS